The Financially Intelligent Parent

8 STEPS TO RAISING SUCCESSFUL, GENEROUS, RESPONSIBLE CHILDREN

June 2007

Dear Amanda,

Thanks for all you do for ADL!

Best wishes,

Eileen Gallo

Jon Gallo

The Financially Intelligent Parent

8 STEPS TO RAISING SUCCESSFUL, GENEROUS, RESPONSIBLE CHILDREN

EILEEN GALLO, PH.D., AND JON GALLO, J.D.

New American Library

New American Library
Published by New American Library, a division of
Penguin Group (USA) Inc., 375 Hudson Street,
New York, New York 10014, USA
Penguin Group (Canada), 10 Alcorn Avenue, Toronto,
Ontario M4V 3B2, Canada (a division of Pearson Penguin Canada Inc.)
Penguin Books Ltd., 80 Strand, London WC2R 0RL, England
Penguin Ireland, 25 St. Stephen's Green, Dublin 2,
Ireland (a division of Penguin Books Ltd.)
Penguin Group (Australia), 250 Camberwell Road, Camberwell, Victoria 3124,
Australia (a division of Pearson Australia Group Pty. Ltd.)
Penguin Books India Pvt. Ltd., 11 Community Centre, Panchsheel Park,
New Delhi - 110 017, India
Penguin Group (NZ), cnr Airborne and Rosedale Roads, Albany,
Auckland 1310, New Zealand (a division of Pearson New Zealand Ltd.)
Penguin Books (South Africa) (Pty.) Ltd., 24 Sturdee Avenue,
Rosebank, Johannesburg 2196, South Africa

Penguin Books Ltd., Registered Offices: 80 Strand, London WC2R 0RL, England

First published by New American Library, a division of Penguin Group (USA) Inc.

First Printing, June 2005
10 9 8 7 6 5 4 3

LIBRARY OF CONGRESS CATALOGING-IN-PUBLICATION DATA:

Gallo, Eileen.
The financially intelligent parent : 8 steps to raising successful, generous, responsible children / Eileen Gallo and Jon Gallo.
p. cm.
Includes bibliographical references and index.
ISBN 0-451-21528-1 (trade pbk. : alk. paper)
1. Parents—Finance, Personal. 2. Parenting. 3. Child rearing—Economic aspects. 4. Money—Psychological aspects. 5. Responsibility in children. 6. Life skills. I. Title: Raising emotionally aware and financially responsible children.
II. Gallo, Jon J. III. Title.
HG179.G2647 2005
332.024'.00855—dc22 2004027478

Printed in the United States of America

To our children, Valerie, Donald and Kevin,
and our grandchildren, Emily and Joshua

ACKNOWLEDGMENTS

This book could not have been written without the encouragement, assistance and nagging of a lot of very bright people who were extraordinarily generous with their time, talent and advice.

We start with Stuart Ende, whose brilliance helped us explore the psychological and emotional issues of children and money; Jilliene Schenkel, for providing a living example of a charitable family; Joel Schwartz, for pushing us unmercifully to write a book accessible to all parents; and Valerie Olvera, a one-woman focus group for keeping us centered.

Then there is our cheering section, for their constant encouragement and suggestions: Sherry Brent, Zo Byrnes, Jerry Florence, Susan Beacham, Wendy Darby and Sharon Dunas.

For sharing anecdotes, experiences and ideas: Barbara Wilson, Larry Mantle, Penny, Art and Scott Antolick, Roz Anderson, Andy Kahn, Dr. George Brumley, Mary Lowengard, Barbara and Phil Hartl, Matthew Kahn, Kathleen Brown, T. J. Florence, Susan Kahn, Jean Chatzky, Karen Florence, Tracy Baxter, Stephan Poulter and Al Wroblewski.

Bruce Wexler, who again helped us focus; Michael Bourret, our agent, for representing us so well; and Tracy Bernstein, our editor, for deciding that *The Financially Intelligent Parent* should see the light of day.

CONTENTS

The Financially Intelligent Parent

8 STEPS TO RAISING SUCCESSFUL, GENEROUS, RESPONSIBLE CHILDREN

INTRODUCTION

Through the Gallo Institute, we have put on seminars and workshops for thousands of parents on a wide range of topics: clarifying money values, talking to children about money, developing a work ethic, the role of charity in raising responsible children and so on.

We start our programs on children and money by asking three questions:

1. *Are you satisfied with your own financial education when you were growing up?* The typical response from the audience is a resounding *no.*

2. *Do you want your kids to get a better financial education?* This time the typical response is an equally resounding *yes.*

3. *How many of you know how to give your children a financial education that helps them develop good money relationships and life values?* The response: *silence.*

People don't have an answer for this last question because no one has ever taught them how to help their children develop good money relationships and life values. They may not even realize how profound the connection is between what they say and do regarding money and their children's future success and happiness. Beyond teaching children how to balance a checkbook or avoiding spoiling them, most parents aren't particularly conscious about their money behaviors . . . which is a shame.

If you want your child to become a successful, ethical, giving human being, you'll develop this consciousness. In fact, money consciousness is at the heart of financially intelligent parenting. Financially intelligent parents are consistently alert for teachable moments. They watch for opportunities to communicate about money with their kids through both their words and their actions. They also possess the skills to communicate effectively. They know how to involve the family in charitable work to communicate their values and how to use allowances to foster a sense of responsibility.

While financial intelligence also involves teaching children about money management, that is not the point of this book. Yes, it's important for children to learn how to budget their money and understand investments. Far more important, though, is what they learn through your money behaviors about what's important in life. You can teach them to be generous through involvement in volunteer activities. You can help them appreciate the difference between spending to meet a real need versus spending to impress others. Your attitude about your job—and the balance you've struck between working for meaning and working for money—can foster a healthy work ethic in your children.

RAISING KIDS WITH MONEY IN MIND

Some parents lack the ability to create an internal structure for themselves and their children that allows them to use money in healthy ways. We've helped many parents develop this structure, and this book will help you do likewise.

The Financially Intelligent Parent, therefore, is an outgrowth of our life's work. We'd like to share with you the paths that led us to this work and how they culminated in this book.

We are a husband-and-wife team with three adult children and two grandchildren. Eileen has a PhD in psychology and is a licensed psychotherapist in Los Angeles, where her practice concentrates on issues related to money. Jon is an attorney in Los Angeles, where his practice is devoted exclusively to estate planning. We began working together in 1986. We had been married the year before; Eileen had a son by her first marriage and Jon had a son and daughter by his first marriage. We were "remarried with children." If you want to give your marriage a real test, just try working together!

One Sunday morning, Eileen read a book review of Susan Littwin's *The Postponed Generation: Why American Youth Are Growing Up Later.* Littwin proposed that an entire generation of young people were postponing the responsibilities and autonomy of adulthood. As parents of adolescents and as professionals, we had started to deal with some of those issues, and Littwin's book served as the stimulus for us to write our first collaborative work, an article that appeared in the proceedings of the UCLA Estate Planning Institute. Soon we began coauthoring other articles combining psychology and estate planning.

When Eileen decided to go back to graduate school to get her PhD, she selected for her dissertation topic the emotional issues involved in sudden wealth. Eileen undertook a two-year study that involved numerous interviews with families who had won the lottery, received a surprise inheritance or otherwise become suddenly wealthy. Several of the parents she interviewed asked some variation of the question, "How much money does it take to ruin a child?"

When we examined the literature on children and money, we found that the books fell into two categories: ones designed to teach kids the basic skills of money management, such as how to balance a checkbook, and anti-money books that offered suggestions (often quite good ones) about what parents could do once their children had been harmed by their parents' money. Over the years, though, we had worked with parents who had done a great job raising kids despite—or maybe even with the help of—their affluence. How had they done it?

We spent about three years of research, interviews, client work and reading to come to the conclusion that money has never harmed a child: What does the damage is money without values!

The result was our first book, *Silver Spoon Kids: How Successful Parents Raise Responsible Children,* published in early 2002. In it we pointed out that the key to raising responsible, emotionally healthy kids in an affluent environment required demystifying money, avoiding the traps that produced feelings of entitlement and elitism and so on. *Silver Spoon Kids* was the ideal book for our client base, which included families on the Forbes 400 list of the wealthiest people in America.

Over time, however, we expanded our client base, finding that an increasing number of middle-class parents were attending our workshops and requiring counseling services. It became clear that they, too, had money issues involving their children, that they were concerned about how their money attitudes and behaviors affected their children and wondered how to help them develop a work ethic. As we worked with these parents, we realized that this was an even bigger topic than the one we had covered in our first book.

We became convinced that we needed to write a second book for a broader audience when we were on the East Coast conducting a workshop for a wealthy family. Everyone was staying at the same luxury hotel, and the hotel had provided a van to take all of us to dinner at a local restaurant. On the way back to the hotel, we were talking to one of the family members about how to structure an allowance for his seven-year-old. The driver turned around and asked for the name of our book because he was facing the same issues with his seven-year-old!

As we looked over client files and conducted research for this book, we made a major breakthrough that was missing from the first book. Though we had provided readers of the first book with many suggestions on how to raise responsible, emotionally healthy kids, we could now identify the eight key behaviors of financially intelligent parents:

1. Encourage a work ethic.
2. Get your own money stories straight.

3. Facilitate financial reflection.
4. Become a charitable family.
5. Teach financial literacy.
6. Be aware of the values you model.
7. Moderate extreme money tendencies.
8. Talk about the tough topics.

WHAT TO EXPECT FROM THIS BOOK AND HOW TO GET THE MOST OUT OF IT

The behaviors just listed provide an accessible strategy that parents of all income levels can implement. As you'll see, we've devoted one chapter to each behavior, providing interactive exercises, checklists, and other information that will help you understand what the behavior entails and allow you to put it into practice. At the start of each money-behavior chapter, you'll also find a financially intelligent brainteaser. These brainteasers encourage you to think about parenting and money in fresh ways, posing child-raising dilemmas that require you to assess your relationship with money.

You'll also find many stories drawn from our work with families. Some of the stories are funny while others are touching. Some illustrate mistakes parents make. Some demonstrate how to be a financially intelligent parent. In all the stories, we have changed the names of the participants. In some cases, we have changed locations and jobs. Many of the stories are composites drawn from our joint experiences.

Prior to the eight money-behavior chapters, we'll give you an overview of why every parent should be aware of and knowledgeable about parenting issues involving money. We'll start by profiling a few financially intelligent parents and describing the principles or beliefs under which they operate. Next, we'll look at the dark side—financially unintelligent parenting and its signs. Right before the money-behavior chapters, we'll explain why financial intelligence is such a crucial commodity for parents in this day and age.

Throughout the book, we'll share the psychological basis behind our concepts and the studies that reveal the importance of parenting with money in mind. There is an overwhelming body of evidence suggesting that parents who have bad relationships with money—who have significant problems in the areas of money use, acquisition and management—can negatively affect their children's emotional growth. We've also looked at classic child developmental stages and found that if parents say and do the right things relative to money at each stage, they can have an overwhelmingly positive effect on their kids.

The theme that runs throughout these pages is that anyone can become a financially intelligent parent. The knowledge, inspiration and tools contained here should help you achieve this goal. Be aware, though, that it will be easier for some of you to implement the book's lessons than for others. Obviously, if you have serious money issues—if, for instance, you're abnormally frugal—you're going to have to work harder than someone who has less significant problems with money. Any parent, though, can incorporate at least some of the money behaviors into his or her parenting style. It will help if you are consistently aware of your money behaviors (especially around your kids), if you identify your particular money weakness and if you adopt a flexible attitude toward how you deal with money-related issues—this last point is the subject of the book's final chapter.

When we wrote our first book, we figured that we might as well get some kind of a return on the cost of our youngest son's bachelor's degree in English; we asked Kevin to proofread the galleys. He did a good job, but we also got busted. When he had finished, he asked us why we were telling parents to do things we hadn't done and not to do things we had done when he was growing up! We replied that we wished we had learned the lessons of our first book when our kids were younger. It would have helped us avoid a number of mistakes. We've learned even more in the past few years. *The Financially Intelligent Parent* is the book we wish someone had written when our kids were young. We hope that you will benefit from our mistakes, our research and our ideas to become a truly financially intelligent parent.

1

THE MONEY BELIEFS OF FINANCIALLY INTELLIGENT PARENTS

We all want to raise kids who are happy and successful, but we often mistakenly think that money is the key to that happiness and success. In fact, the amount of money parents possess has little to do with how children turn out. The attitudes and actions of parents around money issues, though, have a tremendous effect.

On the positive side, parents who exhibit healthy money behaviors communicate strong values to their children. When parents talk openly and constructively about financial issues, avoid engaging in frequent money battles and use their financial resources to help the disadvantaged, children learn lessons about respect, love and giving.

On the negative side, "bad" money behaviors can inadvertently distort the values parents want to communicate; they also make their children tremendously unhappy. Repeated fights about money may communicate to kids that money isn't worth having because it is the cause of anger, hostility, resentment and tension. When parents are workaholics who are rarely home, they communicate that making money and supporting an affluent lifestyle are more important than having meaningful family time.

Financially intelligent parents know how to emphasize the positive impact and minimize the negative one. They understand that money itself is neither good nor bad; it's what they do with it and what they teach their children about it that are important.

Becoming this type of parent is a function of awareness and effort. You need to be aware of the beliefs and practices that define financially intelligent parenting and then resolve to translate this awareness into action. We'll start you on the path to becoming financially intelligent by detailing the seven beliefs of parents who display this quality, but first we'd like to introduce you to three adult children and show you the impact their parents' money behaviors had on them as they were growing up.

THE LONG-TERM EFFECTS OF HOW PARENTS HANDLE MONEY ISSUES

Lauren and Craig, age nineteen and age twenty-four, are personally, socially and financially responsible young adults. Lauren, a sophomore in college, and Craig, an insurance company employee, display remarkable maturity when it comes to acquiring and managing money. Neither of them has ever bounced a check or maxed out a credit card. Each has demonstrated the ability to budget money earned from their jobs and to distinguish between what they really *need* and what they merely *want*. Though Craig isn't earning a lot of money yet, he donates small amounts to an environmental group involved in a cause he cares about. Lauren has a part-time job. Both Lauren and Craig have a lot of friends and are generally happy with their lives. It is not that they don't have issues—Craig is considering other careers besides the insurance industry, and Lauren was upset recently when she broke up with her boyfriend—but they cope well. Though both of them are ambitious in terms of their careers, becoming rich isn't what drives them. For instance, Craig is content to live in a relatively modest apartment, and Lauren drives a six-year-old car. Though they aspire to improve their lifestyles, they aren't obsessed with this goal.

Their parents, John and Lydia, own a graphic arts business that does well but not great. While raising Craig and Lauren, they worked hard at jobs they loved, and though there were some tough times economically, they rarely complained when things were tight. They also made an effort not to engage in arguments in front of Craig and Lauren about money or other matters. Though John tended to spend money more readily than Lydia, and Lydia was in charge of managing the family's money (John had no interest or talent in this area), they established mutually acceptable roles, rules and responsibilities early on that helped them get the bills paid on time and avoided uncertainty or panic over what they could afford. When Craig and Lauren each turned fifteen, their parents got them a prepaid credit card, which they would load each month with their allowance. The kids saved their receipts, and once a month, when the credit card statement came, their parents reviewed it with them. They didn't preach or criticize, but they did use the statement as a catalyst for money discussions. For instance, they asked whether their kids felt that they got their money's worth for each purchase. Looking back, Craig described the process of the monthly credit card review as "a drag." But he added, "I see the benefits. It helped me think through how I was spending money."

Claire, unlike Craig and Lauren, has had a much more difficult, less happy life. Now twenty-six, Claire possesses a number of good qualities, but she also has been in and out of trouble since adolescence. In high school she used alcohol and drugs extensively and twice was arrested for underage drinking; she dropped out of two colleges and never received her degree. Though she eventually secured a sales job with a family friend's business and did quite well for almost two years, she spent money as fast as she made it. She was especially fond of designer clothes, and even though she knew she couldn't afford what she bought, she rationalized her purchases and believed that no harm would come from them. Last year, she was forced to declare bankruptcy.

Claire's parents, Jim and Audrey, exhibited money behaviors that could be described as chaotic. Though they both had good jobs—they made considerably more money than John and Lydia—they were also incapable of managing their money wisely. More than once, Jim lost a large amount of money investing in get-rich-quick schemes. He was constantly looking for and talking about ways he could make a great deal of money, and Claire remembers that dinner table conversation often revolved around money-making ideas and Jim's anger when his investments didn't pan out. Audrey showed disdain for money tasks she felt were "beneath her." She never balanced her checkbook, and she communicated to Claire that "life is short, so why waste it worrying about money." Unfortunately, Audrey also didn't worry about paying bills on time, and Claire remembers at least two occasions when their electricity was turned off because of nonpayment. She also remembers shopping with her mother and seeing Audrey pull out a credit card and say, "I hope the credit card gods like us today." If the card was rejected, Claire would be terribly embarrassed, but Audrey would simply pull out another card and say, "Give this one a spin."

Obviously, John and Lydia were financially intelligent parents, and Jim and Audrey were not. Other factors besides money behaviors influenced how their children turned out, but we've seen these same patterns occur in hundreds of other families. Bad money behaviors often produce troubled kids. Good money behaviors often produce happy, hardworking kids. This doesn't mean that you can never have an argument with your spouse about money or that you have to be the most charitable creature on the planet. At times, even the most financially intelligent parent does or says something that is a mistake. At times, we all spend money on trivial things or miss a bill payment. Occasionally, all of us are dysfunctional in at least one financial area. The goal isn't to be perfect, but to try to establish greater awareness of how you think about and act around these money issues.

THE SUM OF YOUR BELIEFS AND BEHAVIORS

As we saw in the example of Jim and Audrey, the beliefs we communicate about money, as much as our actual behavior, affect our children deeply.

Are you a financially intelligent parent? Answer the following questions to help yourself make this determination:

1. *Do you have unresolved issues around money? Are you a spendthrift, a miser, a chaotic manager of money?*
2. *Do you have goals and a plan to educate your kids about financial matters?*
3. *Do you ever consider the values that you are communicating through your money behaviors?*
4. *Are you uncomfortable talking about financial subjects with your kids?*
5. *Do you have difficulty saying no when your children ask for money?*
6. *Do you use money as a bribe to get your kids to do what you tell them?*
7. *If you feel like you've been neglecting your kids, do you try to make it up to them by buying them things?*
8. *Do you frequently fight with your spouse about financial subjects in front of your children?*
9. *Do you harbor extreme money beliefs, such as money is the root of all evil, or money is what makes people happy?*
10. *Are you neurotically fearful of going to the poorhouse even though you make a good living and there is no basis for this fear?*
11. *Do you ever talk to your children about the importance of giving money to those less fortunate than your family or involve them in a charitable activity?*
12. *Do you give your kids a consistent allowance?*
13. *Do you understand the emotional meaning of money in your life?*

14. *Do you frequently make disparaging remarks about people who are poor or are less successful than you are?*
15. *If your child raises a money issue, do you usually make the effort to take advantage of this teachable moment?*

Answers of a financially intelligent parent:

1. No
2. Yes
3. Yes
4. No
5. No
6. No
7. No
8. No
9. No
10. No
11. Yes
12. Yes
13. Yes
14. No
15. Yes

Few parents receive perfect scores on this questionnaire. If you've never given much thought to these issues, the odds are that you had a number of "wrong" answers. Financially intelligent parenting isn't an inherent skill. Our own parents' money issues combined with societal attitudes have shaped our money beliefs and behaviors, and they have not always shaped them in ways that benefit our children.

But before we can address any problematic behavior around money, we first have to tackle our beliefs about money. Our research has shown that financially intelligent parents

- *are optimistic about their ability to change money behaviors;*
- *value the difference between financial savvy and financial intelligence;*
- *think long and hard about the meaning of money in their lives;*
- *consider the financial education of their children a primary parenting responsibility;*
- *recognize that their unconscious money deeds have at least as much impact on their kids as their conscious money words;*
- *feel that* no *and* enough *are words that children need to hear as part of their money education;*
- *want their children to work more for a sense of satisfaction than for money.*

Let's look at each of these beliefs and attitudes a little more closely.

Financially Intelligent Parents Are Optimistic About Their Ability to Change Money Behaviors

When we pass away, our children inherit our money; during our lifetimes, they inherit our beliefs about money. A financially intelligent parent understands that money history doesn't have to repeat itself. Your children don't have to inherit your anxieties or problems related to money.

In other words, financially intelligent parents believe that both they and their kids are not locked into a behavioral pattern, that even if they've exhibited negative behaviors in the past, they can change in the future. They also believe that their children are capable of adjusting and outgrowing bad attitudes, that they aren't doomed to be forever greedy, entitled or careless when it comes to money.

We can't overemphasize this related point: Financially intelligent parents understand that it's never too late to start! We've helped parents of adult children successfully change their money behaviors, and their kids have responded positively.

Helping children become financially literate takes time and patience. You're going to feel frustrated in trying to encourage your preteen to be less materialistic. You might be upset with your teenager when he displays little empathy for those less fortunate than himself. Similarly, you're going to find some of your ingrained money attitudes and behaviors hard to shake. People who have been obsessively cheap for thirty years, for instance, will have to struggle to display a healthier attitude toward spending, especially in the presence of their children.

The good news is that optimistic parents usually succeed at changing their behaviors and helping their children change. They don't give up when their children do foolish things or when they find themselves falling into old patterns. They persist in the belief that with patience and practice, financial intelligence is possible for them and their children.

Financially Intelligent Parents Value the Difference Between Financial Savvy and Financial Intelligence

Being financially savvy means that you handle your finances well. You budget appropriately, save for retirement, invest intelligently, avoid credit card debt and pay your bills on time. But you may be totally oblivious to the messages about money you are sending your children. Financially intelligent parents tend to be financially savvy, but even if they are not, they are aware of what they are teaching their children about money.

One parent we know, for instance, was socially conscious and involved in a variety of charitable organizations. He was also very smart about spending his money carefully and saving wisely, and he did a good job of teaching his children budgeting, investing and other financial skills. This man, though, was savvy rather than intelligent. He showed absolutely no balance, lecturing his children from the time they were toddlers about "wretched excess" and the need to live simply; refusing to buy products and services from at least half of all businesses because of sins real or imagined; and moaning about how Americans are terribly wasteful and consume far more goods and services than is necessary.

Almost predictably, one child reacted by living even more ascetically than her dad, creating problems at school, where she had trouble making friends because she chastised the other children for being greedy and selfish. The other child responded by rebelling, becoming extremely materialistic and constantly telling his dad that when he grew up, he wanted to make a lot of money and have all the things that he'd been denied as a child. This parent might have been very smart about money, but he did not possess financial intelligence.

Financially Intelligent Parents Think Long and Hard About the Meaning of Money in Their Lives

To many of us, money represents far more than just a medium of exchange. It represents our deepest emotional needs for love, power, security, independence, control and self-worth. Money might represent a scorecard, a measure of success, a source of satisfaction or security, or a cause for anxiety, guilt or dependence. Financially intelligent parents work at understanding what money means to them because they know that their relationship with money will have a profound effect on every aspect of their children's lives.

Financially intelligent parents maintain a money consciousness. They make an effort to think about what messages they are sending their kids regarding financial issues. They don't turn down requests for a toy or insist that their child get a job without thinking about it. They develop a reflex by which they reflect upon and question how their money decisions or responses might affect their child's development. Obviously, they don't do this every second of every day, but they do it often enough that they are alert for mistakes they're making or ways their children are being adversely affected.

We've found that parents are more likely to think long and hard about money when they understand its enormous emotional influence. Sociologist Louis Yablonsky points out that

- *money often forms the basis of our self-concept, self-esteem and sense of intelligence, as well as our perceived status;*
- *we spend our entire time at work focused on making money;*
- *sexual attractiveness is enhanced by the possession of money and diminished by its absence;*
- *money is at the heart of many family fights;*
- *money is a prominent feature in daydreams and fantasies;*
- *money symbolizes power and autonomy.*

Money, therefore, is far more than a medium of exchange, and when parents grasp that it is a symbol for everything from love to success, they take the time to think about what it really means in their lives.

Financially Intelligent Parents Consider the Financial Education of Their Children a Primary Parenting Responsibility

Financially intelligent parents *do not* treat this education as something that can be taken care of through one dinner table discussion or by explaining how a bank account works. One financial birds-and-bees discussion isn't sufficient. Financially intelligent parents view financial education as a continuing process. Whether the subject is allowances, car insurance shopping or credit cards, financially intelligent parents actively seek opportunities to involve their kids in financial learning experiences, taking advantage of teachable moments throughout their children's lives in a variety of circumstances. It may be a small child's innocent question about why houses cost so much or a teenager's complaint that the fast-food restaurant where she works doesn't pay her enough. Parents see these questions and complaints as catalysts for increased financial literacy.

Prioritizing a child's financial education sometimes means making an effort to engage in difficult discussions—a key behavior of financially intelligent parents addressed in depth in chapter 11. For too many parents, money remains the last taboo topic. They are often far more comfortable talking about their sex lives or marital problems than disclosing how much they make or what money means to them. It's easy to rationalize why their kids don't need to know about certain topics such as the compromises they've made to make decent incomes, or to avoid their children's questions about why their cousins have a lot more money and toys than they do.

When financial education is a priority, on the other hand, parents understand that these questions and discussions are their responsibility. As a result, they not only don't avoid them but actively seek them out.

Financially Intelligent Parents Recognize That Their Unconscious Money Deeds Have at Least as Much Impact on Their Kids as Their Conscious Money Words

We are communicating to our children about money all the time. Sometimes the communication is verbal and intentional, such as when we have discussions about allowances or summer jobs. Other times our children absorb messages about money from our behavior, such as observing the way we treat the sales clerk at the department store or seeing us put money in the Salvation Army kettle at Christmastime. Research shows that as much as 90 percent of communication is through nonverbal modeling behavior: what we do, the tone of our voice, our gaze, our gestures and our posture.

Understanding this concept helps us make the unconscious conscious. Financially intelligent parents recognize that they are sending the wrong message when they fail to give a food server or a taxi driver an adequate tip or when they talk about how they wish they could have been the one to make a million dollars through insider trading.

While none of us can catch and control all our negative messages, the goal is to catch and control some of them.

Financially intelligent parents also understand that they may be sending their children money messages because of unresolved issues from their own childhood. In *Parenting from the Inside Out*, Dan Siegel and Mary Hartzell point out that experiences parents have with their children often trigger the parents' unresolved, leftover issues from their childhood. When such an issue is triggered, they experience what psychologists call *implicit memories.* These memories are recalled so fast that it feels as if they are happening right now rather than in the past, and thus they trigger the childhood feelings that accompanied the original experience. Here is an example of how implicit memories can affect the money messages children receive.

Larry and Mary have a fifteen-year-old son, Chris. When Larry was a child, his father became angry and emotionally abusive if Larry ran out of allowance money before the end of the week and asked for an advance. Larry's dad would scream that he was going to be a failure when he grew up because he couldn't manage money. Larry said that when his father yelled at him like this, he would feel rejected, fearful and angry. When Larry and Chris have disagreements over money, Larry sometimes experiences that disagreement as a personal rejection, rather than as a teenager reflexively rejecting his father's advice. The feeling of being personally rejected triggers Larry's memories of his own father, and he becomes angry and fearful.

Emotions such as anger, fear and rejection interfere with our ability to use our prefrontal cortex, the part of the brain that allows us to be rational and reflective. As a result, we end up sending the wrong messages to our kids in these moments. Like Larry, we might respond to our child's reasonable request for money—summer music camp tuition, for instance—by worrying about the cost and making our child feel guilty for no reason. If we repeat this type of behavior regularly, we may raise a child who feels guilty about spending money on herself for any reason!

The belief here, that their unconscious money deeds have a tremendous impact on their kids, helps parents think before they act, especially when it comes to money issues. Financially intelligent parents spend a few minutes at the end of each day asking themselves why they reacted the way they did and whether their behaviors expressed their values.

Financially Intelligent Parents Feel That "No" and "Enough" Are Words That Children Need to Hear as Part of Their Money Education

Under the mistaken notion that they can never give their children enough, some parents shower their children with gifts at all ages and routinely give in to pleas and demands for more. They may set limits in other areas of a child's life, but when it comes to money, they just can't say no.

Sometimes this is due to guilt—they're trying to compensate for being away from home so much, a common problem among parents pursuing high-powered professional careers. In other instances, limit-averse parents are responding to a childhood in which their parents always said no. They want to give their children what they never had, and as a result, they believe in indulging their children with few if any limits.

It is easier to say no in theory, of course, than when staring into the eyes of a child you love who acts betrayed and hurt when you say no. Recognize, however, that the importance of limits is psychologically sound. In all areas of their lives, kids need limits. As much as they might act as if they don't want them—especially in adolescence—they actually crave boundaries. These boundaries give them a sense of security; that security structures their lives and helps them deal with the complexities and uncertainties of growing up. Though kids often push against these boundaries and sometimes cross them, they also need them. Allow children to have anything they want and you foster a sense of entitlement and diminish their drive to achieve. In fact, overindulged children tend to lack a sense of self-worth: They believe that they are not important enough for their parents to bother to set limits.

The art of saying no is one that financially intelligent parents master. It is an art because they must balance the *noes* with *yesses*. There are times when kids deserve rewards and should be allowed to exercise financial independence. A belief in saying no, however, gives parents the inherent right to set limits when necessary. As a result, they don't feel like they are being mean or withholding love when practicing financially intelligent behaviors.

Financially Intelligent Parents Want Their Children to Work More for a Sense of Satisfaction Than for Money

Children who are passionate about a given activity or interest exhibit what social psychiatrists call *autotelic* behavior. *Autotelic* is a word composed of two Greek roots, *auto*, which means *self*, and *telos*, which means *goal*. An autotelic activity is one we do for its own sake, because to experience it is the main goal. In other words, autotelic behavior is behavior we engage in because we enjoy it, rather than for a reward or out of fear of failure.

When we use money to motivate our children, we are creating external motivation rather than relying on their own enthusiasms and passions. As psychiatrist Ed Hallowell points out in *The Childhood Roots of Adult Happiness*, we want motivation to come from the inside and not be supplied from the outside. "You may still deal with carrots and sticks, but if the carrot and the stick come from within a person, that system will last much longer than if the motivation comes entirely from the outside." Hallowell believes that using money to motivate children is as likely to produce a depressed adult as it is to produce a materially successful one.

Social psychologist Mihaly Csikszentmihalyi, who coined the term *autotelic*, points out that the less parents rely on external motivators and the more they concentrate on helping their children become internally motivated, the happier their children will be. If you overemphasize the importance of money or rewards in achieving a goal, rather than the process of achievement itself, you run the risk of turning your child into a kind of money junkie who has no true enthusiasm for anything except more money. This is not a recipe for a meaningful or happy life.

University of Southern California economist Richard Easterlin, who has pioneered studies on the relationship between material goods and happiness, observed in a *Los Angeles Times* interview that the more we make, the more we want. Using money as a motivator simply makes us want even more. If materialism is our motivating factor, we can never get ahead of our material wants. Social psychologists call this the *hedonic treadmill.* The hedonic treadmill ensures that very few of us can be very happy for very long if what motivates us is getting more. As Easterlin comments, "The more you have, the more you need, especially if someone you know already has it." Money and material goods are external; happiness is internal.

A belief in working for passion more than for money helps parents keep kids off this treadmill. The more you can help your child discover what he loves to do and then encourage him to do it, the more autotelic your child will become. Autotelic children are able to keep money in perspective. They view money as a tool to use, not a goal to achieve. They take money into consideration when making decisions, but they don't allow their lives to be driven and controlled by money.

THE EVIDENCE FOR A NEW SET OF BELIEFS

If some of the seven beliefs proposed here make you uncomfortable, don't feel you have to embrace them immediately. We trust that as you read the stories and learn the lessons contained in the following pages, you'll naturally come to make them your own. As you view them within the context of your own childraising, you'll see how much sense they make. We have found that it takes a combination of information and experience before people fully subscribe to all these beliefs.

We also realize that some of these beliefs may run counter to what you've believed for years or to the way you were raised. It is difficult to believe that your child should work for love rather than money when you grew up in a poor household and your parents worked two jobs so they could send you to college. Throughout your adolescence, they may have harped on the disadvantages of being poor to the point that wealth became your sole goal.

If you have a problem with any of the beliefs, all we ask is that you keep an open mind about them. Remember, too, that these beliefs are in the best interest of your child. After years of working with thousands of parents and their children, we've found that resistance to these beliefs melts when parents see how they benefit their kids. It is much easier to subscribe to the belief that kids should work for love more than money when you see your child blossom as she finds a hobby or area of interest that truly excites her. As you'll discover, the more you learn about your child and money, the more credible these seven beliefs will be.

2

FINANCIALLY CLUELESS PARENTS: RECOGNIZE THE SIGNS

Being a financially clueless parent has repercussions well beyond spoiling your children or causing them to be careless with money. If you and your spouse are financially clueless, your children will pay the price in more ways than one. When they are younger, they may be selfish. As teenagers, they may fail to develop a work ethic and ambition, max out credit cards or be overly materialistic. They may also engage you in continuous and emotionally draining arguments over money issues. When they are adults, they may be terrified of taking risks or take too many foolish ones, and they may turn into cheap, superficial individuals.

And this is just the tip of the iceberg.

It is impossible to catalog all the negative repercussions of bad money behaviors. Understand, though, that they are varied and numerous and affect kids from the time they are toddlers all the way through adulthood. Our goal here is to make you aware of how some of these behaviors manifest themselves at specific ages. We're going to put all this within a child development framework, so you can be conscious of what your *money task* is at each stage (relative to your child's developmental task) and how your child may respond if you fail to fulfill your task. In this way, you will become more conscious of how your money words and actions can affect your child's development. This money-behavior consciousness is something all financially intelligent parents learn to develop.

GOOD, SUCCESSFUL PEOPLE CAN BE FINANCIALLY CLUELESS PARENTS

If you're financially unintelligent, it does not mean that you are a bad person or that you've spent your life hovering on the brink of bankruptcy. You might have a great job, have money in the bank and be a good parent in many respects. When it comes to being a financially intelligent parent, though, you're clueless. Despite your intelligence in other areas of life, something causes you to short-circuit when it comes to spending, acquiring or managing money and talking about these issues with your children. To help you grasp the repercussions of being financially clueless, let's look at three generations of one family. As you'll discover, the sins of the father and mother are indeed visited upon the son and daughter.

Harvey and Jane met in 1960 when they were in their twenties and working in sales for a company manufacturing electrical components. Their parents had lived through the Great Depression and were quite frugal as a result, but neither set of parents talked much about money. The one time Harvey asked his father how much money he made, he was told, "That's none of your business." He never asked his parents about money again. Starting when he was about eleven, Harvey received an allowance tied to doing chores. Jane recalled that she "just learned" that money wasn't a topic suitable for discussion. Jane's parents didn't believe in allowances, but they did believe in rewarding good grades; Jane received five dollars for each A on her report card and two dollars for each B.

Harvey and Jane were married in 1965 and had two children, Brad, born in 1967, and Marilyn, born in 1970. Jane quit her job shortly before Brad was born and has been a full-time stay-at-home mom. Harvey worked for an electrical supply company for several years and started his own very successful wholesale distribution company in 1975.

They were warm, supportive parents. Harvey and Jane viewed their own parents as "control freaks" when it came to money, and they were determined not to treat their children the same way. So, rather than having chore-based allowances or paying for grades, they determined to provide their kids with the best of everything. If the kids needed money for school events or to go to the movies with friends, they got it with no questions asked. If they had their hearts set on a particular toy or article of clothing, Harvey and Jane bought it. They were not required to do chores. In fact, they had very few responsibilities except to stay out of serious trouble.

Brad had a bit of difficulty meeting even this modest requirement. Before he reached adolescence, he was caught shoplifting twice, something that neither Harvey nor Jane understood since they gave him everything he wanted. In high school, Brad was involved in a number of incidents, including smoking on school grounds, fights with other boys and mouthing off to teachers. He wasn't a particularly good student, but after a few false starts—he flunked out of two colleges—he managed to take enough business courses to convince a friend to become his partner in a software company. When the business failed, Harvey and Jane provided him with the funds to start a restaurant. When that failed, they bankrolled him again to buy a franchise instant-printing business. A few years later, the printing business went into bankruptcy and Brad was again asking his parents for financial support at the age of thirty-five. During this time, Brad also married and divorced twice.

Unlike Brad, Marilyn's childhood was relatively calm. She didn't get into trouble and did relatively well in school. Marilyn, however, was sullen and withdrawn during much of her adolescence. A talented artist, she spent a great deal of time alone in her room painting grim scenes of death and destruction. Much to Jane's disappointment, Marilyn was uninterested in clothes, preferring basic black for all occasions. In fact, she rejected what she referred to as her parents' "crass materialism" and insisted on attending a local junior college that she could pay for on her own by working as a waitress. She eventually went on to the state university and received undergraduate and graduate degrees in art history. After graduating, she worked as an assistant art curator at a local museum but quit after two months because the job wasn't sufficiently challenging and the pay was "insulting." After living at home for a while, she obtained a position as an art history instructor at a junior college and moved in to her own apartment. It was in a run-down neighborhood, and Harvey and Jane encouraged her to find a better one in a better neighborhood, but Marilyn refused. She also refused to buy a better car than the one that Harvey called "a rolling death trap." Though she saved quite a bit of her salary, she refused to spend any of it on vacations, clothes or entertainment for reasons that escaped her parents and that Marilyn couldn't explain except to say that she believed in living a simple life. Ironically, Marilyn had become as frugal as Harvey's and Jane's parents without the excuse of living through a major financial depression.

Harvey and Jane made mistake after mistake when it came to their money behaviors. From their willingness to give their children everything to their unwillingness to help them develop a sense of financial accountability, they sent messages that encouraged Brad's irresponsible behaviors and Marilyn's antisocial frugality. While other factors certainly contributed to the type of people Brad and Marilyn became, their parents' unconscious money words and deeds played a significant role. They were financially clueless. If they had been financially intelligent, they would have known not only what to do regarding their money behaviors, but when to do it.

MONEY-RELATED MISTAKES DURING A CHILD'S DEVELOPMENT

In the 1950s, psychoanalyst Erik Erikson identified a sequence of eight developmental stages that we all go through from birth to old age. Five stages occur during childhood; completing them successfully contributes to healthy personalities.

The *trust* stage runs from birth until about age two. A child's task is to develop a view of the world as a safe and secure place.

The *autonomy* stage runs from about age two to age four. Here—during the "terrible twos"—children are beginning the long, hard job of becoming self-sufficient and autonomous, separate from Mommy and Daddy. The need for autonomy explains why a child's first two words are probably *mama* and *dada,* and the third is *no*!

The *initiative* stage lasts from about age four to age six. During this stage, children are learning to explore the world and test their limits. Their curiosity about everything is boundless, and their favorite word is *why*.

From about the start of school at age six to adolescence at age twelve or thirteen, children are in the *industry* stage, where they need to develop a can-do approach to the world.

The *identity* stage runs from the start of adolescence until young adulthood. We used to think that young adulthood started around age eighteen. Today, studies show that many young people do not reach adulthood until twenty-six years of age or even later. During this final stage of childhood, children need to develop a sense of their own identity, independent of their family and their family's money.

Through our work at the Gallo Institute, we have identified a parallel series of parental money tasks that will help children grow up with a healthy relationship to money. Conversely, parents who are unaware of or ignore these tasks may be encouraging their children to embrace negative attitudes and actions.

The following chart provides a capsule view of these money tasks:

Child's Age	Child's Developmental Task	Parent's Money Task
0–2	Trust	Provide context
2–4	Autonomy	Help child differentiate among liking, wanting and needing
4–6	Initiative	Talk about money
6–12	Industry	Discuss work ethic, allowances and charity
12–adult	Identity	Teach child about checking accounts and credit cards; launching

Let's look at each of the five developmental stages and the role that parental money behaviors play in each.

Trust. Your parental task during this first stage of life involves helping your children develop context, by which we mean helping them learn to view the world as a safe and secure place. At first, it may seem unlikely that this task has anything to do with money. However, it actually has a profound impact on the attitudes your children eventually develop toward money. To help you understand how this is so, consider that psychologists tell us that we project the sense of security or insecurity we develop during this first stage of life onto three aspects of adult life: food, sex and money. An insecure relationship with any of these three things can cause otherwise sane and sensible adults to exhibit truly bizarre behavior. Anorexia and sexual addiction are just two examples of food- and sex-related abnormal behavior. Gambling, bankruptcy and the like are money-related examples.

The way you create safety and security is by ensuring that your child establishes a strong, continuous relationship with a loving caregiver. Child psychologists call this individual an *attachment figure* and talk about the need for children to have a secure attachment with their primary caregiver. While the mother is often the attachment figure, this certainly doesn't mean that a father or a grandparent can't fill this role. In fact, even loving nannies or daycare workers can serve as good attachment figures.

This attachment doesn't happen, however, when you and your spouse are often absent and you change nannies three times during your child's first two years. It also doesn't happen if the primary caregiver is physically there but emotionally distant. And it doesn't happen if this caregiver is fulfilling this role every other week—she is loving and involved for a week and then is gone traveling for work the following week. In these instances, babies develop feelings of insecurity, which may manifest themselves later in life in regard to food, sex or money—or all three. When parents fail to make sure a secure attachment takes place, they increase the odds that their children will grow up with money-related issues—being overly materialistic, unable to manage money and so on.

Autonomy. Starting around age two, most children start watching television. What do they see? One day in February 2004, we counted the commercials on the Nickelodeon channel from 9 A.M. to 11 A.M There were twenty-nine, promoting everything from toys to fast food to video games. We know some parents who try to insulate their children from the media, but it is usually a losing proposition. If kids aren't exposed to commercials at their own home, they will view them at friends' homes. It's normal for kids to like and want things. Commercial television, though, will start teaching two- or three-year-olds not only that they should like and want what they see on TV, but that they *need* what is advertised.

A parent's money task during this stage is to help kids learn the difference between liking and wanting things and needing everything they see advertised. The former is normal; the latter is not. When you think about good versus bad parental money behaviors, realize that kids learn not only by what we say and do, but also by what we don't say or do. If you use the television as a babysitter and don't sit there, watch with your children and talk to them about what they are seeing, you are allowing slick and motivational advertising to deliver a "you need everything we're selling" message. A steady diet of commercials during this developmental stage likely will yield kids with an overwhelming need for instant gratification. These are the children who will resent you for not buying them things and carry this resentment and anger about what they don't have into adulthood. Financially intelligent parents, therefore, ration the amount of television small children watch and try to watch with their kids whenever possible. In this way, they can help them learn to understand what commercials are telling them and give them the tools they need to evaluate the truthfulness of what is being said. Financially intelligent parents also reframe the way their children think about commercials. Reframing allows your kids to think in terms of "I like" what I see on television, rather than "I need" or "I want" what is being advertised.

Initiative. During the initiative stage, kids become curious about many things, including money. For this reason, parents must become comfortable communicating to their children about financial issues, using both words and behaviors. Financially clueless parents communicate poorly or not at all. Perhaps the worst sin parents commit during this stage is to engage in constant quarrels with each other in their children's presence. As a result, kids grow up associating money with hostility and disagreements, and this association colors their own attitudes about both relationships and money. It can cause them to replicate this behavior when they're older and in relationships, or it may cause them to avoid any discussion about money with their spouses. It can also create a sense of money as the root of all evil and cause kids to pursue interests and careers precisely because they're guaranteed not to make any money at them. Financially intelligent parents learn to keep the majority of their money arguments private. Later in this chapter as well as in ensuing chapters, we'll talk more about how to avoid money fights and settle money disagreements without resorting to harsh words or actions.

During their child's initiative stage, financially intelligent parents also make an effort to satisfy their child's curiosity about why things cost what they cost, even if the questions their child asks seem silly.

Finally, they don't hide money matters from their kids on the assumption that they are too young and won't understand. They talk about salaries, bills, charitable donations and contemplated purchases when their kids are present. Even if their children don't understand every part of the discussion, they learn that their parents view money as emotionally neutral, that they don't overvalue or undervalue it.

Industry. During this stage, financially intelligent parents practice very specific money behaviors. They help their child develop a work ethic and teach the basics of money management through allowances. It seems simple, yet parents are frequently clueless about allowances! Perhaps the most common error parents make is to link chores and schoolwork to allowances. Connecting chores to allowances teaches children that they have a right to be paid for doing tasks that are their responsibility as members of the family. Similarly, paying for grades substitutes external rewards for the internal motivation that helps children grow into self-reliant and happy adults.

You probably know kids who are highly irresponsible and who come to view any request for household assistance—from taking out the trash to mowing the lawn—as an unfair imposition. Later, these same kids may not feel responsible for achieving good grades or doing anything beyond the minimum at a job. They often lack motivation and can become overly dependent on Mom's and Dad's generosity, since they have never learned to value a job for its own sake.

Parents should also be involving their children in charitable activities during this stage. When they don't use some of the family's resources—both money and time—to help people in need, they miss out on an opportunity to teach children that there are uses for money other than consumption. This is a crucial life lesson, and this is the stage when it can really hit home with kids.

Identity. This is the final stage of childhood, and parents model money attitudes and actions here that can prepare kids to function as emotionally healthy, financially responsible adults when they leave home. Sociologists and psycholgists refer to the process of helping young adults go forth into the world standing on their own two financial feet as "launching." Financially intelligent parents use checking accounts, debit cards and prepaid credit cards to teach their children about credit and money management before they get to college. These parents also help their kids learn that money cannot buy happiness, a lesson that adolescents often find difficult to accept. Financially intelligent parents make a conscious effort to avoid frequent displays of extreme money behaviors—greed, extreme frugality or chaotic money management—that may send the wrong message to their kids.

Financially clueless parents, on the other hand, see nothing wrong with these extremes. They may refuse to even discuss most money issues with their children, misguidedly shielding them from the basics of money management. We know one parent who was convinced that teaching his son about checking accounts and credit cards would cause him to become overly materialistic. At the other end of the spectrum, some parents placate their adolescent children with money and material goods. They attempt to make a depressed teenager feel good with an expensive gift or buy an angry adolescent's love with a car. These are the worst things parents can do during the identity stage, unintentionally instilling poor values in their sons and daughters.

HIDING, LYING, OVERBUYING AND OTHER STRANGE MONEY BEHAVIORS

Most of us make at least some of the development-stage mistakes just discussed because we have "issues," ranging from serious psychological conditions to garden-variety neuroses. As parents, we generally try to keep these issues from hurting our children, and our awareness of our vulnerabilities and problems often helps us limit the damage. When it comes to *money* issues, however, we are not as aware of the damage that we are doing. We don't grasp that our obsessiveness about knowing how every penny is spent or how our fascination with the rich and famous is adversely affecting our children. As a result, we don't place governors on our money behaviors as we might on other negative actions of which we might be more conscious.

We routinely see clients whose presenting symptom is some type of money-related behavior. Most of the time, though, these symptoms reflect an underlying emotional issue. Once people understand the underlying issue, they are much better able to manage their negative money behaviors.

Depression, for instance, can emerge in a variety of money attitudes and actions. We had a client we'll refer to as the Gadget Guy. As soon as he became aware of a new electronic gadget, he ordered it. As you might imagine, his house was filled with flat-screen televisions, MP3 players, personal computers and the like. Married and the father of two young boys, Gadget Guy was on a high whenever he brought home a new device, but his exhilaration didn't last long, and he and his wife had terrible arguments at the end of each month when the bills arrived. Many times, these fights were in front of their children. Just as significantly, the children observed their father buying electronic devices he really didn't need and the family couldn't afford and deriving more joy from them than he derived from interactions with family members. If the Gadget Guy's behavior had continued, he would invariably have communicated a warped sense of what was important in life. Fortunately, he dealt with the underlying depression that was causing him to overvalue these toys, and he learned to manage these behaviors.

Some parents suffer from deep-seated anxieties, formed unconsciously when they were children. They may have grown up in a family where Mom and Dad were constantly in money trouble and the creditors were sending threatening notices weekly. They may have had a parent who was overbearing and intrusive, monitoring their every expenditure or other money transactions. As a result, they developed bad money habits.

The Clothing Concealer, for instance, was married with two teenage daughters. She had a responsible middle-management job with a large corporation. She loved to buy clothes, but early in her marriage, she had fights with her husband, who felt that she was spending too much money. Several years ago, she obtained a credit card in her own name and had the statements sent to her office. The Concealer went shopping, sometimes with her daughters, and used the secret credit card. But she couldn't wear the new clothing, because her husband would notice. Over time, she accumulated thousands of dollars worth of new clothes and hid them in the trunk of her car or in a closet in the spare bedroom. Because her children were aware of her secret purchases, they were receiving negative messages about both money and relationships.

This hiding behavior is more common than you might think. *Working Women* magazine conducted a survey of a thousand professional women in 1995 and reported that 13 percent had a secret stash hidden from their husbands. If you've been divorced, the likelihood of a hidden account increases. A 1999 study by the Stepfamily Association found that 71 percent of the women who were married for the second time kept money hidden from their husbands. Lying about purchases is another common but bad money behavior. In a poll taken by *Reader's Digest* in 2001, 40 percent of respondents admitted lying to their spouses, with the most frequent lie being covering up the purchase price of an item. In and of itself, these money lies and hidden accounts might not seem so terrible. Consider, though, what it communicates to children about marriage and trust. When children are aware that one of their parents is hiding money or purchases from the other—especially when they become aware in an early developmental stage—they associate money with guilt and taboos and are taught that relationships don't have to be open and truthful.

Being aware of money behaviors that are sending your kids the wrong messages is one way to help yourself manage these behaviors. Though you may not be able to eliminate them, you can certainly learn to shield your children from them as much as possible. Remember, it's the frequent repetition of these behaviors that causes the most harm. To help create this awareness, look at the following list of money behaviors and ask yourself the following questions:

- *Am I guilty of this behavior?*
- *Do I repeat this behavior frequently?*
- *Do I often behave in this way when my children are present or within earshot?*

- *How might this behavior negatively affect my child during each developmental stage?*

Potentially Negative Money Behaviors

- *hiding money/accounts from my spouse*
- *lying to my spouse about what I've spent money on*
- *buying certain products or services obsessively*
- *talking incessantly about being one step from the poorhouse when this is not the case*
- *exhibiting a fascination with the rich and famous (watching television shows, buying magazines, gossiping about celebrities)*
- *spending a great deal of time coming up with get-rich-quick schemes that never pan out*
- *using credit to obtain a lifestyle far beyond my means*
- *being completely irrational about purchases in a specific category (e.g., buying luxury automobiles when I can't pay my mortgage, or refusing to spend money on decent clothes even though I have plenty of money in the bank)*
- *paying cash for everything, or refusing to own a credit card or get a loan, even when I am well-off financially*

TWO TELLTALE SIGNS OF FINANCIALLY CLUELESS PARENTS

Perhaps the two biggest signs of financial unintelligence are arguing constantly about money-related matters and routinely "gambling" with family money. These behaviors will undermine two crucial developmental tasks. When you argue all the time, you are not providing your child with the safe and secure place that is crucial during the trust phase. When you take foolish risks with family money, you are failing to send the proper message about hard work and responsibility that is important during your child's industry stage.

Arguments About Money

Certainly arguments are part of every marriage, but these arguments don't have to be a constant in a child's life. While it doesn't hurt children to see their parents occasionally disagree about money, frequent, name-calling fights about the same money issues ("You spend every penny I make!" and "You're a cheap SOB!") cannot help but have a negative psychological effect, especially if they take place month after month, developmental stage after developmental stage. The key, therefore, is to make a conscious effort to manage and minimize money arguments in front of the kids. This is not always easy to do, of course, because arguments can flare up quickly and uncontrollably. Money arguments can be complex, and we'll devote more attention to this topic later, but for now recognize that constant money fights don't just harm your marriage, they also hurt your child. We've found that keeping this simple fact in mind can help moderate the severity and lessen the frequency of these fights.

Gambling with the Family's Wealth

Gambling with the family's money doesn't only mean betting the house in a high-stakes poker game. We have counseled adults who have placed their families on precarious financial footing for all sorts of reasons and in all sorts of ways. Some are day traders who never thought they would lose money in the market. Some quit their jobs and failed to support the family because they wanted to pursue some personal vision such as sailing around the world or because they just wanted to drop out for a while. There are parents who spend huge amounts of money on "toys"—fancy cars, boats, travel—and end up struggling to cover the costs of the necessities. Invariably, these gambles end up creating great anxiety in children, especially when the car is repossessed, when they are pulled out of activities parents can no longer afford and when the resulting money problems create constant fights. Children develop a sense of inevitability of loss that affects not only their financial life but also their personal life. They come to believe that they are not in control, that they are at the mercy of forces larger than themselves. This can produce long-lasting emotional trauma in children that may even spiral into depression.

We've had a number of adult clients whose parents gambled with the family money. Tanya, for instance, came to us when she was thirty-three, a professional woman with a good job who was depressed, unable to spend money and having difficulty sustaining meaningful relationships. During most of her childhood, her father kept trying to start new businesses. Some succeeded for a while before failing, while others failed immediately. Tanya's mother worked and kept the family afloat financially, but at a high emotional cost—Tanya witnessed numerous fights between her mom and dad about his harebrained schemes. She vowed that when she grew up, she would never allow herself to be in a position where she couldn't support herself. As a result, Tanya grew up with a compulsive need to save money. Although her income was close to eighty thousand dollars a year, she lived in a furnished apartment, bought her clothes at thrift stores and felt that she could not afford to take vacations or socialize with friends by going to restaurants or movies. She lived in fear that history would repeat itself and that she, like her father, would not have enough. Just as significantly, she was terrified of relationships with men, convinced that she would inherit her mother's role and that the men would prove to be good-for-nothings.

If you find that one or both of these money behaviors applies to you, one of the first and simplest steps you can take is to create a Money Constitution for your family. The Money Constitution is a basic agreement about how you and your spouse are going to spend and manage money. For example, you might agree that any non-routine expense over five hundred dollars requires the approval of both you and your spouse. You might also agree that any disagreement will be handled in private after the kids have gone to bed. As part of the constitution, agree that there will be no secret stashes of cash or credit. Along with these family financial laws, however, your constitution should also be flexible, so you can include amendments that take your specific family circumstances and money styles into consideration. For instance, one amendment might provide for separate checking accounts because you balance the checkbook to the penny and your spouse is constitutionally unable to balance it. If you then decide to have one joint account as well—a common plan in many families—then you must agree on what percentage or amount of your joint income should be deposited to the joint account. Talk about the constitution with your children. This process teaches them that money is an appropriate topic to discuss and that there are rational and appropriate ways to resolve differences over money.

SIGNS OF POTENTIALLY NEGATIVE MONEY BEHAVIORS IN CHILDREN

Financially intelligent parents pay attention to their children's money behaviors as well as their own. They are observant about behavioral money patterns in their kids that suggest that something is wrong. Though they don't overreact to a few instances of greediness or any other negative behavior—what child isn't guilty of refusing to share with a sibling or being overly materialistic at times?—they treat negative money patterns seriously.

One of the best ways to spot these patterns is by viewing them through the developmental stage lens.

Autonomy. Watch for signs that your child is exhibiting the dreaded "I needitis." For instance, your child says he "needs" everything he sees advertised on television. He doesn't express this just once or a few times, but routinely. In addition, this expression isn't just a mild wish but a demand, a fierce commandment for you to buy this toy or that one. Frequency of expression combined with intensity of need is cause for concern.

Initiative. Some kids never talk about money. Others make it the sole topic of conversation. Reluctance to engage in money talk may have to do with the money fights you have with your spouse or your confusion and frustration trying to manage money. If your child makes money the sole topic of conversation, take a look at your own behavior. Do you talk about anything else?

Industry. Watch for signs of indolence or an unwillingness to pitch in around the house without the promise of a financial reward. Again, recognize that all kids in this preadolescent group will exhibit this type of behavior occasionally. When children frequently demand money in exchange for their labor or resist your attempts to get them to do yard work, to do the dishes or to help out in any way, then something else is going on. If you've been linking an allowance to chores and paying for grades, you're probably contributing to your child's financial illiteracy. Similarly, if your son or daughter refuses to participate in charitable activities, you should be concerned.

Identity. Are your children picking fights with you about money issues? Do they max out their credit cards and need to be rescued? Do they lack passions in life, from music to skateboarding to reading to art? Teenagers without passions are like boats without rudders. They need strong interests during adolescence to grow into competent adults. If your children are financially irresponsible, angry about money or generally apathetic, these are signs that something is wrong.

Here is what the parent's money task chart looks like when we add the signs of financial illiteracy in children:

Child's Age	Child's Developmental Task	Parent's Money Task	Sign of Financial Illiteracy
0–2	Trust	Provide context	Not applicable
2–4	Autonomy	Help child differentiate among liking, wanting and needing	"I needitis"
4–6	Initiative	Talk about money	Never talks about money; only talks about money
6–12	Industry	Discuss work ethic, allowances and charity	Absence of charitable impulses; expectation of rewards for helping around the house; laziness
12–adult	Identity	Teach child about checking accounts and credit cards; launching	More fights over money issues; maxing out credit cards; lacking strong interests

3

WHY NOW: THE FACTORS THAT INCREASE THE ODDS OF MAKING MISTAKES

Most of us try at least as hard as previous generations to be good parents; in fact, we know more about how to be good parents than earlier generations did. Despite this effort and knowledge, we are doing a worse job than any generation in recent history when it comes to practicing good money behaviors. Recent events in the world around us have caused us to act in financially unintelligent ways, ranging from excessive financial anxiety to frantic overspending.

This type of extreme money behavior prevents our children from mastering what psychologists call *emotional regulation*—the ability to manage and control emotions. Without emotional regulation, we would give in to every impulse: We see someone funny-looking and we laugh; we become angry at someone and hit him; we need money and we rob a bank. We teach our kids emotional regulation by giving them tools and techniques that allow them to modify their initial emotional response to a situation. As they learn to regulate their emotions, they create a system of dos and don'ts that become actions. Psychologist Aaron Beck describes the process as creating a series of rules that we learn as children and follow as adults, even though we are not aware of the rule book. For example, when we are watching a movie and experience a scary scene, we don't jump up and run away; we regulate our emotions by reminding ourselves that it is just a movie. When we see a child having a temper tantrum at the toy store, we are seeing someone who probably isn't able to regulate the frustration of not getting what he wants immediately.

Financially intelligent parents help their children modify their initial emotional response in various areas, ranging from consumption to feeling guilty for having too much or feeling angry and resentful for having too little. If parents don't help their children learn to modify their initial emotional reactions in these areas, their children may encounter all sorts of problems as they grow up. When kids don't learn ways to cope with their disappointment, they may react in a self-destructive manner, such as turning to alcohol or drugs to feel better about a bad grade or romantic rejection.

Helping kids learn to cope with a highly consumerist, volatile and "expensive" society is difficult. If, however, we understand and are aware of the major trends that are hampering both our money behaviors and our ability to help our kids regulate *their* money behaviors, we are less likely to be victimized by them. Let's look at the Big Three:

- *the developing role of psychology in selling to kids*
- *9/11 and the economic downturn*
- *the dramatic increase in housing and educational costs*

PSYCHOLOGY AND SELLING TO KIDS

Many authors and psychologists assert that the media rather than parents are raising children today. Before dismissing this assertion as hyperbole, consider some frightening statistics. U.S. consumer spending accounts for around 70 percent of the U.S. gross domestic product. In other words, our entire economy is driven by consumer spending. There was a good reason politicians were begging us to go back to the malls and spend following 9/11.

Advertisers spent more than $200 billion in 2001, or a little more than $2,000 a year to reach each family in America. They were not trying to reach just you; your children represent an extremely attractive target market. About $26 billion a year is spent on advertising to kids, with about half of that spent by the food and drink industries, according to Marion Nestle and Margo Wootan in "Spending on Marketing to Kids Up $5 Billion in Last Decade" (*The Food Institute Report*, April 15, 2002). Children marketing expert James V. McNeal describes kids as "rookies" and "consumers in training" who are "socialized into the consumer role by parents, with help from educators and business."

It's difficult to teach our kids how to regulate their relationship with consumption when someone is spending $26 billion a year to make them want and need everything they see!

Although the experts can't quite agree on how much purchasing power is controlled by kids, the numbers are clearly enormous. The June 28, 2004, issue of *Time* magazine projected that American kids under age thirteen spent at least $40 billion of their own money on purchases from candy to clothes. In 2001, teenagers were estimated to have spent at least $170 billion. *Time* magazine projects that children, one way or another, influence more than $600 billion in purchases. At a conservative estimate, our kids are responsible for almost three-quarters of a trillion dollars in purchases annually.

Given what's at stake, it is no wonder that the advertising industry has become extremely sophisticated about selling to children and has developed psychologically astute marketing techniques. For instance, they know how to encourage children to pester us into buying them things. Advertising industry statistics show that nagging is responsible for about a third of all family trips to fast-food restaurants and purchases of children's clothing or videos. Cheryl Idell, a guru in the field of advertising to children, is the author of "The Nag Factor," an article for copywriters and others who sell to kids. Idell explains that more products are sold when kids whine with *importance* rather than *persistence*. What's the difference? Whining with persistence is being a broken record: "Mommy, I want Barbie's Dream House; Mommy, I want Barbie's Dream House"; and on and on until you are driven to distraction. Whining with importance is giving a reason: "Mommy, I need Barbie's Dream House so Ken and Barbie can settle down and raise a family." As Idell points out to the copywriters, they have to put copy into the ad that gives kids all the reasons they should want the product, and in language they can use to nag their parents.

Advertisers have also become skilled at communicating to children that consumption will make their lives better and that their self-worth hinges on the brand of their possessions. At the same time, they communicate to parents that giving children *things* equals giving them *love*. It's difficult to say which message is causing the greater long-term harm, but together they have a profoundly negative effect on children's relationships with money and our ability to help them learn to regulate their money behavior.

According to the Kaiser Family Foundation, the typical kid is exposed to forty hours of media weekly through a combination of television, radio, magazines, movies and the Internet. Our children typically see between 480 and 770 advertisements a week, or between 25,000 and 40,000 advertisements a year. By the time children are three, they often have become brand-conscious. Our friend Madeline remembers taking her two-and-half-year-old to the market. They were walking down the detergent aisle when her daughter stopped and said, "Mommy, buy that one. It gets your whites even whiter!" A young mother recently told us that when she and her six-year-old passed a new BMW, he yelled out, "Mom, we need that car! It's the ultimate driving machine!" When she told us the story, she commented, "The TV is talking to my kid and telling him what to say to me!"

When marketing professionals are accused of corrupting children's values, many respond that it's the parents' job to provide kids with the right values. But even marketing professionals are starting to get concerned. In a Harris Interactive poll of youth marketers conducted in 2004, 61 percent felt that advertising to children starts too early. Though we believe marketers should be more responsible for the messages they send, we also believe that parents are responsible for monitoring and counteracting the impact of these messages and helping their kids learn to regulate their money behavior. This is a much greater responsibility than it was years ago, but it is one that any parent is perfectly capable of handling with the right knowledge and effort.

We need to protect our kids by instilling positive values and critical thinking, especially when it comes to commercials. This can be done in a number of ways, but here are some simple suggestions every financially intelligent parent should adopt:

Limit Your Child's Exposure to Commercials. If you're watching with your child, turn off the television—or at least turn off the sound—when commercials are on. A recent study by the American Psychological Association found that kids under the age of eight have a tough time distinguishing commercials from entertainment. Encourage your child to spend at least some of her time in front of the television watching rented movies or stations without commercials. Even better, buy a personal video recorder or digital video recorder, prerecord the programs and filter out the commercials. You should also limit the time she spends watching television. The accumulated and repeated messages of advertising are what does the damage. Remember that television is not the only way our kids are being exposed to commercials. Sophisticated Internet sites such as www.neopets.com attract millions of kids under the age of thirteen and offer games in which kids win points by viewing commercials. As a parent, you have the power to limit your child's exposure to commercials.

Counteract Negative Advertising Messages. When you and your child are watching television and a commercial airs that suggests that a brand name can make you happy or successful, explain that this isn't the case. Don't deliver a long-winded lecture; just note that people become happy and successful based on hard work, meeting goals and knowing themselves. You don't have to counteract every commercial you view. Every so often, however, provide your child with some real "truth in advertising."

Capitalize on Teachable Moments Related to Advertising. At some point—usually when you're in a store—your child will see a product featured in a commercial and say he wants it. Ask your child whether he saw a commercial for the product and what happened in the commercial. If it seems like the ad was misleading or manipulative, point out why it was deceptive. Your child may still want the product, but at least you may have instilled some skepticism about the advertising—skepticism that will probably prove justified if you buy the product and it turns out not to deliver on the inflated advertised message. These requests for advertised products provide you with teachable moments, and financially intelligent parents take advantage of at least some of them.

Some parents may have their doubts about the power of advertising over their children. After all, some commercials seem so idiotic and simplistic that it's difficult to believe they have much of an effect. But remember that marketers have become very sophisticated about pushing our kids' hot buttons at each developmental stage.

What's wrong with this? In *Wise Up to Teens: Insights into Marketing and Advertising to Teenagers,* Peter Zollo makes the point that at least half of all ads aimed at teens focus on friendships or romantic relationships and suggest that the product or service being advertised will help make the reader cool. Enmeshed in the identity stage of their lives, teens are trying to develop their own identities, separate from their family. Think of how many CDs, jeans, tank tops and lipsticks you can sell by convincing teenagers that they can attract friends through your product. Even more troublesome, you can create the illusion that the right product or brand name can provide them with a new identity, an illusion that can hinder their development.

Just as disturbingly, the consumerist culture is targeting increasingly younger market segments. For the one-year-old who doesn't have everything, the Teletubbies Web site offers forty items to purchase, ranging from backpacks to dolls to videos to saucers. On its Web site, the American Academy of Pediatrics states it "does not recommend television for children age 2 or younger." For older children, the academy recommends no more than "1 to 2 hours per day of educational, nonviolent programs. . . . The first 2 years of life are especially important in the growth and development of your child's brain. During this time, children need good, positive interaction with other children and adults. Too much television can negatively affect early brain development. This is especially true at younger ages, when learning to talk and play with others is so important."

9/11 AND THE ECONOMIC DOWNTURN

Our world became a much more volatile place after 9/11, and we no longer feel as secure as we once did. The world has become more unpredictable and uncertain. In this type of environment, we become more anxious than ever before, and this anxiety affects our money behaviors. We are much more likely to exhibit extreme behaviors—to be cheaper if we tend toward penny-pinching or to be more extravagant if we tend toward spending—as a response to volatility. For instance, if we feel the world might explode at any second, why not spend all that money on a Ferrari? Because extreme money behaviors, repeated too often, can send the wrong messages to our children and get in the way of their learning to regulate their emotional responses to money and consumption.

We usually don't think of our money behavior as extreme. In a very real way, our money behavior is often a natural reaction to unnatural events and conditions. The term *homeostasis* provides an explanation for these reactions. Homeostasis comes from two Greek words: *same* and *steady*. Our body is always attempting to attain homeostasis. If we get too cold, we begin to shiver. Shivering generates heat and warms us. It's our body trying to keep our temperature steady. If we get too hot, we sweat. As the perspiration evaporates, it cools us. Again, it's our body trying to keep our temperature steady. It's like Goldilocks and the three bears: we don't want it too hot or too cold, too hard or too soft, or too big or too small; we want it just right.

Emotional homeostasis is also important. We don't want to be too high (manic) or too low (depressed). Emotionally, we want to be just right. Our mind achieves emotional homeostasis by regulating our emotions, just as our body achieves physical homeostasis by regulating our temperature. When things are badly out of kilter—physically or emotionally—processes kick in to counteract the imbalance and bring things back to being just right. The events of 9/11 have caused an emotional and economic homeostatic reaction. Fearful of the future, some people responded to the trauma of 9/11 by becoming maniacal personal money managers, continuously checking and rechecking their investments. By knowing exactly where every penny is, they attain some illusion of security. Unfortunately, the cost of this illusion is borne by their children. When they see their parents hunched over the computer every night tearing their hair out and muttering darkly about an unbalanced checking account, they may adopt these same extreme behaviors or rebel and embrace the opposite extreme. Or they may grow up with a sense of fear and a lack of security that will affect them in other areas of their lives.

For others, 9/11 produced excessive spending. Within a few weeks after 9/11, businesses and politicians turned to Madison Avenue for help. Gene DeWitt, former chairman and chief executive officer of the advertising agency Optimedia, commented that "retailers should be promoting—not just advertising, but promoting like hell, because the consumer needs to be given reasons to spend." Automakers offered financial incentives, often with patriotic themes. Airlines, cruise lines and Las Vegas resorts and casinos offered 50 percent–off sales. Politicians got into the act by telling us that we needed to demonstrate our patriotism by getting back to the shopping malls.

We're not suggesting that there is anything inherently wrong or deceptive about linking patriotism with consumerism, only that it has had a negative impact on some parents' money behaviors. Some became alarmed at the call for more spending, deciding that the government knew more than it was saying and that a major financial crisis was just around the corner. Others decided to heed the call and began buying their children all sorts of things, justifying behaviors that they might otherwise realize would result in spoiling their kids. All these messages add up to situations where we are not teaching our kids to regulate their emotions, because we are overreacting or reacting in other inappropriate ways.

Consider how your money behaviors have been affected by some of the events just described; the following questions should help:

- *Have you dramatically increased your spending or your saving since 9/11?*
- *Do you talk more about your money worries in front of your kids than you used to?*
- *Has the prospect of being downsized out of a job caused you more than one sleepless night in which you dwell on your ability to pay for your child's education, meet mortgage payments, retire when you planned and so on?*
- *Has your child asked you why you talk about money so much or whether there will be enough money for something she wants?*
- *Have you made a major move—downsizing your lifestyle, moving to a new home, changing careers—in response to the volatility in the world and your sense of insecurity?*
- *How have the swings of the economy affected your attitude toward charity? Are you less likely to give money to charities or to homeless people you pass on the street?*

THE INCREASED COSTS OF HOUSING AND EDUCATION

The costs of housing and education probably present the most direct challenge to parents attempting to practice financially intelligent behaviors. All parents want their kids to grow up in safe neighborhoods and go to good schools. Until relatively recently, most middle-class parents could achieve this goal. Today, however, housing in many neighborhoods has become outrageously expensive, and not only have college costs gone through the roof but many parents are also shelling out for private school, sometimes starting in preschool. As a result, some moms and dads unbalance their financial behaviors, giving too much emphasis to the type of house and community in which they live and the school their kids attend. They may become nervous wrecks trying to maintain mortgage and education payments, communicating to their children that it is acceptable to allow money to make them a little bit crazy.

Some parents don't become nervous wrecks but instead become workaholics. They labor long and hard so they can afford a home in an upscale neighborhood or send their child to a private school. When their children act like they don't appreciate the sacrifices their parents have made, parents might say, "You don't know how lucky you are." Their children can grow up feeling guilty. If their parents are always worried about money and talking about how difficult things are, they may grow up with a conscious or subconscious aversion to hard work, since such workaholism clearly has not made their parents happy. These workaholic parents may also be absent parents, and the children are raised primarily by childcare professionals or relatives. Again, we're not suggesting that there is anything wrong with two-working-parent households, but when both parents work excessively, they become vulnerable to all sorts of financially unintelligent behaviors. They are more likely to substitute money (e.g., gifts) for love or not engage in the types of activities (dinner table conversations, trips, etc.) where they can communicate their values through money-related discussions. If you have only one or two meals with your children weekly, the opportunity for consistent conversation is lacking.

There are also parents who have no choice but to live in modest apartments or homes and send their children to public schools. Some of them become bitter and resentful that they can't afford more, and this bitterness and resentment is communicated to their children. They make snide comments about families who send their children to private schools and complain about inequities in salaries and inherited wealth. In this environment, children may grow up feeling deprived and may come to believe that making a huge amount of money is the only recipe for happiness.

In recent years, costs of housing and education have increased dramatically, and both parents and kids are feeling the stress. Take Robert and Becky, for example. Robert owns his own business and makes close to one hundred thousand dollars a year. Becky worked for an advertising agency until the birth of their first child and then became a full-time stay-at-home mom. Two years ago, when their children were eight and six, they bought a nice home in a somewhat upscale neighborhood with well-regarded public schools. Although their house payments increased by almost eight hundred dollars a month, they felt that it was a good investment and that there was no need for Becky to go back to work. For the first year or so, they were happy with the kids' school. During the second year, though, they became increasingly dissatisfied with the teaching as well as the environment of the school. Both their children had teachers who were mediocre at best—one was nearing retirement and seemed to have lost interest, and the other was very young and inexperienced, allowing the class to spin out of control. In addition, there were a few bullying episodes among the older kids at the school, and Robert and Becky felt that the administration was not handling the situation properly. They also heard horror stories—primarily involving drugs and sex—about the district's middle school that their children would be attending. They decided to send both their children to private school, with a total tuition cost of thirty thousand dollars a year. Now, of course, Becky had to return to work.

Robert and Becky aren't the only parents under financial pressure. Let's examine some statistics that reveal how serious the situation has become.

The Joint Center for Housing Studies of Harvard University publishes an annual study, *The State of the Nation's Housing*. The 2003 report discloses that since 1991, housing prices have risen faster than mean household income throughout much of America. In large measure, we believe that this increase in housing prices is attributable to parents looking for homes in safe neighborhoods (generally, the suburbs) with good schools. The Joint Center reports that between 1997 and 2001, the number of households spending more than half their income on housing has increased by seven hundred thousand. Today, almost fifteen million households are spending more than 30 percent of their income on housing.

Prior to 9/11, a 2000 Gallup poll disclosed that 91 percent of Americans identified education as the single most important social issue facing the country, above the economy, health care and social security. In the post-9/11 world, national security is clearly the most important issue, but education continues to be near the top. A July 9, 2002, article in the *Christian Science Monitor* reported that nearly two-thirds of three- to four-year-olds are attending preschool, up from 4 percent in the 1960s. More alarmingly, preschool costs, especially in major cities, have become exorbitant. Our four-year-old granddaughter's tuition for preschool exceeds what we paid to attend a private college in the 1960s! According to a study by the Children's Defense Fund in 2000, the average annual cost of child care for a four-year-old in an urban area center is more than the average annual cost of public college tuition in all but one state. In some cities, child care costs *twice* as much as college tuition. And this isn't restricted to preschools. A good private college can cost forty thousand dollars a year or more, and the U.S. Department of Education reports that the price of tuition at the average state university, adjusted for inflation, has nearly doubled since 1980.

By taking the following true–false quiz, think about how these higher educational and housing costs make financially intelligent parenting more difficult for you:

1. *My spouse and I each work more than fifty hours in an average week to afford our house and send our children to good schools.* *True* *False*

2. *Our dinner table conversation often revolves around the difficulty of paying for both our home and our children's educations.* *True* *False*

3. *My spouse and I frequently express anger or resentment over people who have inherited money to buy beautiful homes in great neighborhoods.* *True* *False*

4. *We constantly tell our children how lucky they are to live where they live and attend the schools they attend.* *True* *False*

5. *We are house-poor and frequently complain about it.* *True* *False*

6. *We suspect that our children feel guilty because we have paid for them to go to good private schools and live in a safe neighborhood. We often remind them of what we've done for them.* *True* *False*

7. *My wife and I firmly believe that our child is much more likely to lead a happier, more successful life if we send him to the best school in our area.* *True* *False*

The more questions you've answered with *true*, the more challenging it will be to practice financially intelligent behaviors.

The good news is that you can decrease the odds of making mistakes by learning the eight key behaviors of financially intelligent parents. If you integrate these eight key behaviors into your routine and make a conscious effort to apply them to interactions with your children, you will be on your way to raising kids with good money relationships and life values.

4

ENCOURAGE A WORK ETHIC

Financially Intelligent Brainteaser

Your fifteen-year-old daughter is unusually smart and talented and wants to become a professional musician or a doctor. Not only is she an accomplished violinist, but she is extremely talented in the sciences, having taken special college courses during the summer in microbiology. She has never received less than an A in any course. Because she studies so hard and practices her violin so much, she rarely helps out around the house.

What should you do?

A. Allow her to devote all her time and energy to her schoolwork and violin since she needs every spare second if she is going to accomplish her ambitious goals.
B. Jointly work out with her a reasonable number of chores that are her responsibility as a member of the family.
C. Give her a token chore or two every so often so that her siblings don't feel she's the favored child.
D. Explain to her that she is in danger of becoming isolated from the family, and for that reason you're assigning her an hour of chores each day to help her lead a more balanced, family-oriented life.

(Answer at end of chapter)

Kids aren't naturally diligent or naturally lazy. A work ethic is learned behavior, and you're the one who teaches your kids to acquire it. If you're like most parents, you want your children to work hard and derive meaning and satisfaction from what they do. Unfortunately, you may be sending them another message inadvertently. Though you may insist that your kids do their homework and help around the house, these requirements alone don't guarantee that they will grow up with a sense of accountability and a drive to achieve. As we'll see, financially intelligent parents encourage a work ethic in many different—and sometimes surprising—ways.

A work ethic's benefits are multifaceted. Not only does it increase the odds that kids will do well in school and, later, in their careers, but it fosters a sense of personal responsibility. Kids without a work ethic tend to develop into lazy, unmotivated teenagers and young adults, blaming others for their failures.

Developing a work ethic in your children is a holistic process. It's not as simple as making them pick up their toys before they can play outside or forcing them to get a job at the local fast-food restaurant. To help you grasp the diversity of issues involved, we've prepared the following questions. Answer them based on the ways in which you've raised your children (or based on your beliefs about how you will raise them in the future).

- *Do you give your children an allowance tied to doing certain chores around the house?*
- *Do you encourage your children to work hard at school but discourage them from getting jobs because they detract from their time to do homework?*
- *When you give your children a task to do, do they usually take care of it effectively and on time or sloppily and when they feel like it?*
- *Do you expect nothing less than straight As and express disappointment at Bs?*
- *If your child works hard in a class but receives a mediocre grade, do you provide him with positive or negative feedback?*

- *Do you feel it's more important for your child to work during the summer or spend time learning about something she's interested in?*
- *Do you compliment your kids for a job well done, even if it's something as simple as shoveling snow or raking leaves?*
- *Are you more likely to complain about work in front of your kids or to express satisfaction about your job and career?*
- *Would you characterize yourself as lazy and unmotivated when it comes to doing chores? Do you often argue with your spouse about this subject?*

Just pondering these questions gives you a sense of a work ethic's complexities and variables. Throughout the chapter, we'll help you learn the right ways to answer them. This learning starts by defining what a work ethic really is.

A BELIEF THAT TRANSLATES INTO ACTION

A work ethic is more than just putting our nose to the grindstone. It is the belief that we are personally accountable and responsible for what we accomplish (or fail to accomplish), coupled with the concept that what we are accomplishing is worthwhile. A work ethic is a characteristic of both work and play. In sports, this ethic is often mentioned as a trait of good players. Kids with a strong work ethic usually work (or play) hard, do well in school and feel happy and satisfied even if they fall short of their immediate goals; they realize that they are working toward a larger, more worthwhile goal than just getting an A in a class or excelling in one game.

Financially intelligent parents are highly conscious of the need to model behaviors and have conversations with their children that stress this work ethic. From the time their kids are little, they provide them with encouragement and support for their efforts at home, at school and at work. These parents know the positive consequences of instilling a work ethic in their kids . . . and the negative consequences of failing to do so. We've worked with many families that don't have this awareness, and as a result they frequently take the easy way out and allow their kids to slide. Specifically, they

- *permit their kids to get away with not doing their chores because it's too much of a hassle to keep reminding them;*
- *avoid talking to their children about their grades when they perform below their abilities in school because they don't want to get into a big fight;*
- *find a summer job for their kids rather than allow them to seek work on their own.*

To avoid falling into these traps, recognize the dangers of raising an overindulged child. Being overindulged isn't just for the rich. We know many middle-class parents who either are afraid to set rules and enforce them or just aren't paying attention. In the latter instance, they're so focused on their own hectic lives that they don't realize that their child is shirking responsibility or not putting forth a solid effort at school. This can result in a child who is given too much and held accountable for too little. Put another way, kids with a work ethic are developmentally enabled, while overindulged children are developmentally disabled. Let's look at some of the things psychological research has to say about overindulgence:

- Overindulgence produces kids who lack self-assertion, are more dependent, have less concern for others, and are less self-reliant (the more they are overindulged, the more they need to be overindulged). (D.J. Bredehoft et al., *Perceptions Attributed to Parental Overindulgence During Childhood,* p. 16.)
- Overindulgence is not restricted to giving kids too much. Overindulgence also consists of doing too much for them

and having lax rules and no chores. (David Bredehoft et al., "No Rules, Not Enforcing Rules, No Chores + Lots of Freedom = Overindulgence Too.")

- Overindulgence is a more important risk factor than peer pressure in terms of the likelihood that children will abuse alcohol and drugs. (David. J. Wilmes, *Parenting for Prevention.*)

A work ethic is preventative medicine for overindulgence. To understand how this ethic serves as a preventative, let's take a brief look at a critical but relatively unknown study.

THE VALLIANT STUDY

Much of what we know about the importance of developing a work ethic is the result of a successful entrepreneur wanting to discover the qualities of a good retail store manager and a law school professor wanting to study juvenile delinquents.

William Thomas Grant opened his first W. T. Grant Co. 25 Cent Store in 1906 with a thousand dollars he had saved from his work as a salesman. By 1936, in the middle of the Great Depression, his stores were doing over a $100 million a year in sales. Two years later, Grant made a gift to Harvard University to "analyze the forces that have produced normal young men." Until then, doctors, sociologists and psychologists had devoted themselves to studying people who were mentally or physically sick. Now, for the first time, substantial research was being devoted to studying what made people well adjusted.

Between 1939 and 1942, 268 Harvard sophomores were selected for the study. Each went through a battery of interviews with a psychiatrist and a social worker. The social worker then traveled throughout the country to meet the students' parents and secure a complete history of their infant and child development. Twenty of the Harvard students eventually withdrew from the study. For more than sixty years (or until their deaths), the remaining 248 continued to participate. They filled out questionnaires every two years, provided records of physical exams every five years and were reinterviewed about every fifteen years. Their wives and children were also interviewed.

Socioeconomically, the group was diverse. Although a third came from homes in the upper 10 percent of both wealth and income, almost half were attending Harvard on scholarship or had to work during the academic year to support themselves. While about a third of the men's fathers were professionals, half of all the fathers had never graduated from college.

At almost the same time that Grant made his gift to Harvard, Sheldon Glueck, a young professor at Harvard Law School, and his wife, Eleanor, a social worker, obtained funding to study five hundred young men from working-class neighborhoods in Cambridge who had been sent to reform school. They also selected five hundred schoolboys from the same neighborhoods who, at age fourteen, had never been in any legal trouble. The five hundred nondelinquents were the controls to whom the reform-school boys were compared. Both groups came from the same high-crime neighborhoods and attended the same inner-city schools. More than two-thirds of their families had recently been on welfare. Like the Harvard sophomores, the five hundred nondelinquents were studied for more than sixty years.

In 1970 the Grant and Glueck studies were combined, and George Valliant, MD, a psychiatrist on the faculty of Harvard Medical School, eventually became the director of what is now known as the Harvard Study of Adult Development. The two studies make up the longest prospective studies of physical and mental health in the world.

The results of the Harvard Study are eye-opening, especially for parents. In a 1981 article in the *American Journal of Psychiatry*, Valliant reported that the single biggest predictor of adult mental health was "the capacity to work learned in childhood"—in other words, the development of a work ethic. Men whom Valliant described as "competent and industrious at age 14"—men who had developed a work ethic during the industry stage of development—were twice as likely to have warm relationships (with both family and friends), five times more likely to have well-paying jobs and sixteen times less likely to have suffered significant unemployment.

Our experience with thousands of families over the years confirms Valliant's conclusions. Time and again, we've seen the positive impact of a work ethic on children's maturity and success and the negative impact when kids lack this work ethic.

The question then becomes, How and when do you instill this ethic effectively? To answer this question, let's look at the three areas that provide parents with opportunities to teach kids to be industrious and responsible for their work: chores, school and jobs.

MORE THAN A CHORE: GETTING THINGS DONE THE RIGHT WAY

This isn't about treating your children as slaves, piling tasks on their small shoulders and seeing how much they can handle. Neither is it about treating your children as employees, paying them for every chore they complete. Rather, chores are opportunities for kids to learn lessons about life. Financially intelligent parents use chores as ways to help their kids gain self-respect and take pride in a job well done. These are lessons that will ultimately help these kids excel in whatever career they choose. They will learn early on that a job well done is its own reward, and that a parent's compliments and other rewards (getting to go out and play) are secondary benefits. In short, they will be autotelic—they will possess an inner drive to do well rather than be dependent on external motivation.

When your children are three or four, they are ready to handle simple tasks. No matter how long it takes them to learn to master even the simplest of chores—putting their dirty dishes next to the sink so Mommy can put them in the dishwasher or helping Daddy take the garbage out—they are starting to think of themselves as members of a family in which everyone contributes to the whole. These are the kids who are more likely to grow up and be adept at working on teams and establishing productive partnerships.

They also learn to delay gratification through doing their chores. They grasp that they can't go out and play until they clean up their rooms. John Gray, PhD, in *Children Are from Heaven*, ranks learning to delay gratification among "essential life skills," and for good reason. Many of these kids will turn into adults who save their money for something important, such as buying a house or putting their own kids through college rather than purchasing the plasma television or fancy sports car they can't really afford. Being able to prioritize is a gift parents can offer their young children; you'd be surprised by how many parents don't give this gift until their children are teenagers, and by then it's more difficult to learn.

Though it's great if you can come up with interesting chores for your kids to do, mix in some mundane tasks. Everything in life isn't exciting; there are many absolutely necessary but routine chores waiting for us. Tolerating a certain amount of boredom is a life skill. Sometimes you have to sit through a boring course in school before you qualify to take an interesting one. Sometimes you have to work at a boring entry-level job to be qualified for a more challenging one.

With these concepts in mind, review the following eight tips on how to make chores educational, enriching experiences:

1. ***Exhibit a positive attitude when you do your chores.*** *Kids watch their parents like hawks, and they won't miss your sullen response when your spouse asks you to fix a broken doorknob or to go to the store for a gallon of milk. What you say and especially what you do sends a strong message to kids, and even a subtle response—a furrowed brow, an exasperated sigh—will encourage kids to mirror your attitude. You don't have to be phony about it and pretend you can't wait to haul the garbage cans out to the street.*

You can, however, avoid negative gestures that suggest chores are beneath you or something to fight about with your spouse.

2. ***Assign chores to various family members according to interests, or convene a family meeting and let the kids participate in the decision-making process.*** *If your kids are very young and you assign the chores, try to take into consideration their natural talents. Is your daughter nurturing? Have her help feed the pets. Does your son love the outdoors? Have him help you with the gardening. When the children are a little older, have a family meeting in which you outline what needs to be done around the house. Let the kids participate in figuring out the basic chores—from doing the dishes to raking leaves to keeping the family room clean—and who should do them.*

3. ***Do some chores alongside your kids.*** *Family chores become a battleground when kids think their parents are foisting work off on them so they can relax. So pitch in. Communicate that chores are part of everyone's life. Raking leaves or shoveling snow with your children may seem like ordinary activities, but doing them together transforms them into something meaningful and even fun. Shared chores like these also foster a sense of teamwork.*

4. ***Help your children integrate chores into their routines.*** *As your kids grow up, they will have other responsibilities—homework, sports, private lessons—that seem to have a higher priority than household chores. They need to practice juggling the low-priority tasks with the high-priority ones. When they become adults, juggling personal and professional responsibilities, little tasks and big ones, is constant. People who do it well tend to lead balanced, successful lives. Start your kids out on the right foot by teach-*

ing them that they have to allow five minutes in the morning to make their beds and clean their rooms and a half hour on weekends to do some yard work. Show them how they can create a schedule for their week on the computer or by using a calendar.

5. ***Share your chore expectations.*** *Children internalize their parents' expectations; these expectations are usually more powerful than consequences. Let your kids know that you expect them to pick up after themselves, that picking up is just a given in your family. Sharing your expectations provides you with the bulletproof answer when they ask why they have to clean up their room when their friend Charlie doesn't have to: "That's the way we do things at our house."*

6. ***Foster accountability for assigned responsibilities.*** *In other words, you want your kids to feel a sense of accomplishment for doing their tasks the right way and on time; you also want them to recognize that they are responsible for the consequences if they fail to do so. One of the best ways of achieving this latter goal is by linking consequences to the nature of a given chore. If you get stuck trying to figure out how to do this, think of Johnny and his chair.*

   Johnny, age five, was driving his parents crazy by rocking his chair back and forth at the dinner table. Meal after meal, Johnny's parents would first ask him to stop rocking and then tell him to stop. Meal after meal, Johnny kept rocking. And why not? It made him the center of attention and put him in control of what was being talked about. One night when Johnny came to dinner, his chair was missing. "Johnny," said his father, "since you can't use your chair correctly, we've had to put it away." "What am I supposed to do?" asked Johnny. "Eat standing up," replied his mother. After a day of eating breakfast, lunch and dinner standing up, Johnny got his chair back and never returned to his rocking.

If Johnny's parents had threatened to take away his television privileges, the consequences would have been divorced from the action and would have had far less impact. Therefore, if your four-year-old's job is to put his toys away in the evening and he keeps forgetting, the consequence might be that he can't play with them for a few days. You might explain that if he is old enough to take the toys out of the toy box, he is old enough to put them back in before bedtime. If your fourteen-year-old daughter keeps forgetting to empty the dishwasher after dinner, wake her up thirty minutes earlier in the morning to put the dishes away before breakfast.

7. ***Don't link allowances or other rewards to family chores.*** *One of the most common mistakes parents make is paying kids for doing chores, often in the form of an allowance. While you want your children to understand that a job well done receives rewards, you don't want them thinking that they should be paid for fulfilling family responsibilities. This creates a sense of entitlement that can carry over to adult life. When you find an adult who works only for the money—and who refuses to stay one second after 5 P.M. because "I don't get paid any more if I stay late"—then you're probably looking at someone whose parents fostered this sense of entitlement.*

   Financially intelligent parents resolve the paradox of chores and rewards in the following way. They divide chores into two categories: F (family) chores and X (extra) chores. The F group involves routine family responsibilities necessary to keep the household running smoothly, such as washing dishes, taking out the trash, making the bed and so on. The X group involves tasks that you might pay someone else to do: washing the car, mowing the lawn, babysitting a younger sibling. The X group generally requires more time and effort, and kids understand that they are being rewarded for their time and effort rather than for their routine family responsibilities.

8. ***Avoid constant criticism as your child learns to do chores the right way.*** *A hypercritical, judgmental parent who thinks she is instilling a work ethic in her children is going to have exactly the opposite effect. She'll raise kids who resent their chores and try to get out of doing them. If they can't get out of them, they'll rush through their tasks and do a slipshod job, or they'll learn to procrastinate. Constant criticism makes kids feel that they'll never do a good job, so why try? They'll internalize the notion that they're not good enough, and as they become older they may feel the same way about school and jobs.*

    Recognize that kids face a chore learning curve and that they learn at their rate, not yours. Once a chore is assigned or selected, show your child how to do it. If your child makes a mistake, don't rant and rave. Be calm and show him again how to do it, and tell him that the next time, he'll do it right. And when you see him doing it right later on, don't simply accept the result as something he's supposed *to do. Praise him for doing it well. Too many parents notice when their children do something wrong; not enough notice when they do it right.*

    At one of our seminars, Adrienne recalled that when she was five years old, she started helping her mother separate the laundry. She loved the feelings of being helpful and competent. When she was six years old, Adrienne received a new chore: watering the plants in the window boxes on the patio. The first time she watered them, the water pressure through the hose was too high, and mud and water spattered on the windows. Instead of showing her how to adjust the water pressure, Adrienne's mother yelled, "Can't you do the simplest thing right?" Adrienne said that she hated family chores from that day forward.

    Be aware that constant criticism from an older sibling can also do damage. Some rivalry and teasing among siblings is normal. An older brother or sister who is constantly criticizing the way a younger sibling is doing her chores, however, can devastate the younger child. Take the older one aside and ask how she would feel if the roles were reversed and she was the recipient of constant criticism from an older sibling. Most of the time, this is enough. If it isn't, you may simply have to monitor the situation and intervene when the older sibling is being hypercritical.

THE SCHOOL QUESTION: DOING YOUR BEST VERSUS BEING THE BEST

Let's start off with a surprising truth: Pressuring your children to get straight As does not help them develop a work ethic. It may increase their stress to off-the-chart levels, but it won't help them gain satisfaction from achievement or become self-motivated. Elisabeth Guthrie and Kathy Matthews, authors of *The Trouble with Perfect*, note that children need to take chances and possibly fail if they are going to develop a strong sense of self. When parents turn up the pressure on grades, they encourage their children to play it safe in order to achieve a highly ambitious goal. As a result, they're not willing to write a paper on a topic that really turns them on; they'll choose a topic that they think will turn the teacher on. When kids are obsessive about achieving perfect grades, not only are they less willing to take risks, but they're less creative and spontaneous than other children.

Pushing kids too much is a universal problem. An October 15, 2003, editorial in the *Korea Times* discusses how graduates of Seoul University burn out from the intense pressure to achieve at school. The editorial writer advises parents not to "force your children to study too much too fast. Let them go at their own pace. Nobody pushed Einstein, and he turned out all right."

While you want to encourage your kids to work hard at school, your focus should be on motivating them to do their best rather than be the best. Consider the following pairs of be-the-best (B) and do-your-best (D) parental advice:

B: I know math isn't your top subject, but if you study an extra hour each night, you can get an A.

D: *I know math isn't your top subject, but pay attention in class, ask questions if you don't understand and do all the homework, and you'll be fine.*

B: You're not going to get into one of the elite colleges unless you quit spending all your time playing music and focus exclusively on your schoolwork.

D: *You need to find a balance between playing music and doing your homework.*

B: We're spending a lot of money sending you to private school, so we expect your grades to demonstrate you're grateful for this opportunity.

D: *We hope you'll take advantage of the opportunities to enroll in classes and do the type of projects that are unavailable at public school.*

B: It's good that you received a 97 on your fifth-grade English test, but with a little more effort, you could have received 100.

D: *Ninety-seven is a terrific score; tell us what you wrote about.*

B: To be the top student in Mrs. Jones' class, you need to talk to her, figure out what she's looking for and give it to her.

D: *If Mrs. Jones expects you to do a project a certain way, but you feel strongly that there's a better way to do it, that's okay with us, but we suggest that you talk to her about your plans.*

Beyond distinguishing between these two types of advice in your school-related discussions, you can do a number of other things to facilitate a work ethic:

- ***Communicate through your actions that you believe it's important to make a solid effort at school.*** *It's essential that you not just say that you believe it's important, but that you take actions that reinforce what you say. To that end, make sure you create a quiet environment for your child to do his homework—set rules regarding interruptions such as phone calls and online communication. You should also provide your child with resources for doing well at school—dictionaries, encyclopedias, online access for research purposes. Attend school open houses, parent-teacher conferences and your child's school-related activities (sports, plays, music).*

- ***Involve yourself in (as opposed to just observing) your child's schoolwork.*** *This doesn't mean that you should do the work for him, hover over him while he does homework or correct every mistake on every paper he brings home. It does mean that you should make yourself available when he asks for your help. Assist with drills and help him learn to prioritize assignments. Don't just talk about homework, but also ask whether graded papers or projects were handed back, what tests and class projects are coming up and so on. Double-check with the teachers on a periodic basis to make sure that your child is handing in all homework and to find out what grades have been handed back recently.*

  Some parents believe that their children don't want them involved in the school process. Don't believe it! Jacquelynne Eccles, a professor of psychology at the School of Education of the University of Michigan, has studied programs designed to foster parental involvement in their children's schools. Her research discloses that children want *their parents to be involved.*

- ***Initiate conversations about school-related ideas.*** *Too often, parent-child discussions about school revolve around grades. Instead, focus on ideas raised in school. Talk about the subject of an essay your child wrote, or about what motivated her to do a particular drawing, or about her feeling that she should be allowed to do an assignment her way. Your willingness to listen to her as well as respond with your own ideas will demonstrate that you admire the passion and energy she brings to her schoolwork.*

- ***Encourage your children to participate in extracurricular activities that excite them.*** *Some kids aren't particularly excited by their academic classes but exhibit great interest and aptitude in other areas: music, art, computers, sports, ecology clubs and so on. Developing a work ethic around subjects that truly interest and involve kids is important. Certainly, they also need to learn how to work diligently when subjects aren't interesting (just as they need to learn to complete even mundane chores properly), but extracurricular activities offer an avenue to work hard at and take pride in something they relish. When they do participate, be careful not to dismiss or devalue their efforts. Don't say, "I'm glad you enjoy band, but you're probably not going to make your living as a musician, so get your priorities straight." Even if your child doesn't become a musician, his experiences playing in a band will show him how hard work pays off in greater proficiency at an instrument, and he'll take pride in his accomplishments. This is what a work ethic is all about.*

JOBS: HOW TO INITIATE YOUR CHILD INTO THE WORLD OF WORK

Some parents believe that the only way for a child to develop a work ethic is by having a real job. If a family business exists, they put that child to work as soon as she is able to do simple tasks. If there is no family business, parents insist that a child immediately get a job upon turning sixteen and work after school and all summer. Their premise is that nothing teaches a kid to value work like having a real job, a real boss and a real salary.

Other parents encourage their kids not to get jobs. They believe their son's and daughter's job is school, and that they should devote all their time and energy to excelling academically. Summers are for summer school or to pursue private lessons or to relax and reenergize after a grueling school year. The notion here is that children acquire a work ethic in the school environment and that it eventually transfers over to the work environment.

Neither group of parents is wrong, but we've found that there's a middle ground that better suits the needs of most children. While some teenagers are driven to find jobs out of financial necessity and other teenagers are so academically overwhelmed they couldn't work even if they wanted to, most teens can benefit from some exposure to the workplace. Before we talk about teens, though, we'd like to talk about work and your elementary-school-age child.

No, we don't believe in child labor. At the same time, we've found that when kids learn about jobs during the industry developmental stage (six to twelve years old), they tend to have a better grasp of what work means and the choices involved in terms of careers. Perhaps the best resource we've found for kids during this stage is Take Your Children to Work programs. Admittedly, some of these programs are worthless—you take your child to the office, stick her in the corner with her crayons and paper and, except for snacks and lunch, ignore her while you do your job. Over time, however, various groups have become more savvy about how to structure these programs to benefit children.

The Ms. Foundation for Women's Take Our Daughters and Sons to Work program, held annually in April, encourages offices to "adopt" entire classrooms for the day, allowing them to become part of a given office culture for that day and really experience what work is like. The East Central Illinois Women Attorneys Association sponsors an annual mock trial on Take Our Daughters and Sons to Work

Day in which kids serve on a jury and decide whether Rumpelstilskin has a case against Queen Mallory for failure to pay him for spinning straw into gold. At Cardservice International, a large credit card processing firm, kids get to create computer-generated logos, and Cardservice managers evaluate them and pick winners.

If your company doesn't follow an established protocol for kids at work but you want to take your child (and your boss approves), we recommend doing the following:

- ***Start out showing your child what you do.*** *Give him a tour of the workplace and let him see some things you're working on. This will acclimate him, allowing him to appreciate the work environment that until this point he's only heard you talk about.*
- ***Assign him a work-related activity.*** *Obviously, you need to tailor the activity to his age and attention span. It may be something as simple as sorting papers into folders or using the Internet to find information about a work subject. Whatever it is, give him a specific task with a clear goal and time limit.*
- ***Talk to him about the activity.*** *Ask him whether he thought it was easy or difficult. Determine whether he enjoyed doing it. Praise him for what he did well and suggest other ways he might have gone about it.*
- ***Open up about how you do things.*** *Share a work failure and a work success. Let him know how you felt when you got chewed out by your boss for sloppy work. Tell him how great you felt when you came up with an idea that everyone at your company loved.*

In and of itself, one day a year at your office won't develop a work ethic in your children. It will, however, prompt your kids to start thinking about the nature of work and the choices involved. They may also be prompted to ask you questions over time that help clarify these choices. From "Do you really like what you do?" to "How much money do you make?" to "Why do you have to work so late?" their questions (and your answers) will help them get a sense of how work can be a meaningful, rewarding activity. No matter how silly or tangential your child's question might seem, take it as seriously as he does.

Even if you can't take your child to your office for some reason—you work at home, your boss discourages bringing children into the workplace—you can still take advantage of the previous suggestions. If you can't take your kids into the office, bring the office to them. Take pictures or make a video of your workplace, and then share it with your children. You can use the video or photos to inspire a game of "playing office" with your kids. Invariably, these visual aids will stimulate them to ask you the types of questions they would have asked if they had actually visited you at work. If you work at home, your child may be familiar with your work space, but the odds are that you've never taken her beyond the surface of this space; she's seen you typing on your computer keyboard or talking on the phone, but you've left her in the dark about what you were typing or whom you were talking to. Now, let her sit next to you and help type a report or search for information on the Internet. If you have a phone with a speaker, turn it on so your child can listen to the type of conversation you have regarding your work. Again, this will stimulate her to think about what you do for a living and ask questions.

When it comes to teenagers, don't expect them to find a job that might help them achieve specific career goals. While it's great if your daughter wants to be a doctor and she obtains a job as a volunteer in a hospital, most adolescents don't know what they want to be when they grow up, and even if they do, few part-time jobs will help them get there. Instead, teenagers often obtain menial jobs to earn extra cash—cash they use for clothes, dates and so on. Even a menial job, though, can contribute to the development of a work ethic. Your child may not want to grow up to be the manager of a fast-food restaurant, but being an employee of one allows him the opportunity to learn skills that will help him no matter what career he chooses. Whether he's taking orders for burgers or bagging groceries, these jobs call for him to learn how to function as a member of a team, how to interact with customers and how to relate to a boss. Perhaps more significantly, a job is an opportunity for your child to see a direct correlation between his effort and his performance. At school, kids may try hard at subjects that they're not particularly good at, receiving average grades. At work, effort often translates into good performance. Your child will feel a sense of accomplishment when his boss tells him that he did well, even if doing well involved nothing more than getting a customer's order right.

Financially intelligent parents recognize how these menial jobs build a work ethic. Help your children learn from their experience by

- ***treating the job with respect.*** *Don't sneer at the job's tasks or pay or look down your nose at the position. Instead, engage your son or daughter in conversations about hamburger-cooking procedures and shelf stocking without condescension.*
- ***allowing your child to make job decisions.*** *You're going to be tempted to intervene when your child is searching for a summer job or having to deal with a problem at that job. You'll want to tell your kid to choose job A over job B or how to handle a temperamental boss. While it's terrific to offer your child ideas, let her be the decision maker. Allow her to choose the job or figure out how to deal with his boss. Kristen, age seventeen, was working for the second summer in a row as a bagger at a supermarket, and she was doing a good job, filling in when the store was shorthanded and often working beyond her shift when it was busy. She was being paid the same hourly wage she earned the first summer. Kristen felt that she deserved an increase but told her parents she wasn't sure whether she should ask for one, how to ask and when. Her financially wise parents engaged in a Socratic dialogue, asking her questions such as, "What's the worst thing that can happen if you ask for a raise?" Finally, Kristen did ask and was granted a two-dollar-per-hour increase.*

Her parents said they had never seen her prouder of anything she had done.

- ***limiting their hours during the school year.*** *Some kids will want to work long hours because they want money for a car or some other luxury. As a financially intelligent parent, you need to help them achieve a balance between work and school. The teenager who works hard and takes pride in both his schoolwork and his job is more likely to develop a solid work ethic than the kid who focuses on only one area. Limit your child's work time to fifteen hours or less per week during the school year, and that should give him time to achieve the proper balance.*

PLANFUL COMPETENCE

If you need any more motivation to help your child develop a work ethic, consider a fifty-year study by sociologist J. S. Clausen. He found that children who learned what he called *planful competence* in early adolescence had more stable, satisfying careers and fewer midlife crises and divorces as adults. Planful competence means being dependable, having self-confidence and using intellect to solve problems. Kids who exhibit a strong work ethic have these qualities in spades. They learn how to do things right and to think before doing. This helps them avoid the impulsive, thoughtless decisions adolescents are prone to make, and it helps them acquire an area of expertise when they're older.

We don't intend to make a work ethic sound like an exact science. Some kids develop it early and some later. Some may go through a prolonged adolescence of underachievement until a specific event catalyzes their desire for fulfilling work and meaningful success. Some may drift from job to job until they hit upon a field that is their true calling.

As a parent, you can't control these factors. What you can control, though, is how you help your children learn about jobs, school and chores. If they learn to value a work ethic, they will probably use it to achieve success and satisfaction sooner or later.

Answer to Financially Intelligent Brainteaser

Answer A may be tempting for parents who are ambitious for their children, but it communicates the wrong message. It suggests that family is secondary and that a child has no responsibility to the family. Answer C is a bad idea, not only because the other siblings will see through the ruse but because the daughter will get the same message she would get from answer A. Answer D is unfair; you don't want to blunt her drive to achieve by burdening her with an unfair amount of household busywork. Answer B, therefore, makes the most sense. As important as it is to support a child's interests and ambitions, parents must also communicate the importance of family responsibilities, so that the children are contributing, involved members of the family as well as of the school. ◆

5

GET YOUR MONEY STORIES STRAIGHT

Financially Intelligent Brainteaser

Your spouse has found what she feels to be your dream house. It has more room (which you need), is in a great neighborhood with great schools and has an enormous master bedroom with skylights, something you both would relish having after being cooped up in the tiny bedroom in the house you now live in. The problem is its price; it's more than you and your wife agreed you could spend. You're terrified that it's the wrong move, that even if the bank says you could afford it, you would be stretching yourself too thin. Your wife demands that you make a decision right at the dinner table. When you suggest that you should not be talking about this in front of the kids, she says it's their lives too and they have a right to be part of the discussion. When you initially refuse to talk about it, your wife becomes furious, and you know that you're going to lose your temper as well.

What should you do?

A. Dismiss your children from the table and have your fight in private.

B. Allow your children to witness the argument since it will educate them about both sides of the financial coin.

C. Discuss the issue calmly with your spouse to find a compromise that may make you both a bit uncomfortable but that you both can live with.

D. Refuse to talk about it, demonstrating to your children that no financial issue is worth fighting about.

(Answer at end of chapter)

You send your kids messages about money all the time through your words and actions, often without meaning to. If you're married, your spouse is also sending your kids money messages. Quite possibly these money messages conflict with one another. Maybe you're a saver and your spouse or your ex-spouse is a spender. Perhaps your spouse loves to work and values making as much money as possible, while you disdain both work and acquiring money, believing there are more important things in life. As you might imagine, your child is confused by these disparate messages. Even worse, he is going to grow up without clear money values, increasing the odds that he will be susceptible to negative attitudes and money behaviors.

To know what money messages you are sending your kids, you need to get your money story straight. This isn't something you can do without serious thought. If you are married, you need to talk with each other about your money relationships in the areas of acquisition, use and management. Is one of you communicating to your kids that it's critical to save for a rainy day, while the other is saying, "Spend today because you don't know what tomorrow brings"? By talking with each other and revealing your financial beliefs and idiosyncrasies, you are better able to send your children coherent and consistent money messages. This takes more than a five-minute discussion with your spouse. You need to reach agreement on many issues, ranging from allowances and saving for college to how you handle questions from your kids about money. It also isn't limited to what you say about money; you need to walk the walk.

To incorporate getting your money story straight into your repertoire, the first step is understanding exactly what a money story entails.

EVERYONE'S GOT A STORY

Your money story is an open, honest and personal story of your relationship with financial issues, especially as you grew up; most people's relationship with money takes root before adolescence. We have found that it is often easier to understand this relationship with money by putting it in the form of a story. To bring this story to the surface, you must figure out what money meant to you as a child and how this meaning has changed over the years. Answering the following questions will help you write your money story:

- *What did I learn about money from my mother when I was growing up?*
- *What did I learn about money from my father when I was growing up?*
- *Did other people teach me about money when I was a child? What did they teach me?*
- *What money lessons did I learn that were helpful?*
- *What money-related attitudes and behaviors that I acquired when I was growing up have caused me trouble?*
- *How do these experiences—both good and bad—show up in my life today? in my relationship with my children? in my relationship with my spouse?*
- *How do I feel about the impact of these experiences on myself and the people I care about?*
- *Am I satisfied with my financial education?*
- *If I'm not happy with this education, what do I wish were different about it?*

Use your answers to create a capsule bio about yourself and money. It doesn't have to be long or include answers to every question, but it should capture your particular money habits and the origin of these habits. We've also found that it helps to give the story a title and to write creatively. Here is an example:

The Midas Crutch

When I was growing up, my dad worked two jobs to help make ends meet. My mom was sick a lot, so she didn't work, which added to my dad's money worries. He had good reason to worry, but he kept pounding it into my skull that if I didn't want to end up like him, I'd become a doctor or a lawyer. It wasn't that he was bitter about having to work two jobs—his day job was being a store manager, his night job was being a foreman in a factory, and I think he liked both—but he just thought there was a much better way of living, and he wanted me to take advantage of it. He always talked enviously of people who made a lot of money in what he considered cushy jobs. I remember wishing he had one of those jobs so he could be at home more and spend more time with me.

I didn't become a lawyer or doctor but ended up as a vice president with a major corporation. So I make good money, and my wife says I spend it with "reckless abandon," especially on my children. My feeling has always been, if you have it, why not spend it? Maybe this attitude is a result of how my father acted, and that I'm spending for him, in a sense. Even though he died more than ten years ago, I guess I feel like I'm making up for all the things he couldn't buy for himself or our family. When my wife protests that I'm spoiling our kids, I reassure her by saying I can make more in a few years, that people know how good I am at what I do and reward me appropriately. She says I'm financially arrogant, and sometimes I can hear my younger son exhibiting a similar type of arrogance, and I suppose it bothers me—he's always had a privileged life and perhaps doesn't realize that you have to earn the right to talk that way.

By putting your story into writing, you achieve two goals. First, the act of writing makes you more aware of your relationship with money. Second, you can compare and contrast your story with that of your spouse (or ex-spouse if you're divorced). It's quite possible that you don't know your spouse's story, and this exercise will spotlight points of difference. Later, we'll discuss more precise ways to define your stories and the differences, but this is an easy way to get started.

Whatever money story you have to tell, be aware that this story has two points of origin. The first evolves from your parents' words and actions related to money, along with whatever you picked up from friends and the media. (As we've already discussed, the media's primary message today is that consumption is good, buying more will make people happy and the one who dies with the most toys wins.) The second point is how we organize this information in our mind. We all have a distinct way of processing and organizing these money messages and behaviors. Even siblings in the same household are likely to organize their views and their relationships with money very differently.

Because we receive so much of our money story from our families as we are growing up, either we tend to duplicate their money attitudes as adults, or we rebel and exhibit exactly the opposite money behaviors. Holly, for instance, grew up in a family where her parents were truly chaotic money managers. If they had money, they spent it. They were often months late in paying bills and had several cars repossessed. As an adult, Holly is a compulsive saver who lives far below her income level and becomes extremely anxious if she does not pay bills the same day they arrive in the mail. Holly is married to Jack, who lavishes Holly with extravagant gifts and whose attitude toward bills is, "Don't worry; they don't disappear if you forget to pay one on time."

Because opposites really do attract, it's not uncommon for parents to have very different money stories and money styles. This usually isn't an issue early on, and we've found that many people are married for a year or more (or have children) before they realize their money habits are diametrically opposed; or they discover that their spouses have idiosyncratic money habits, such as only paying bills on the second day of the month or a willingness to spend a lot of money on big-ticket items such as cars and houses but an unwillingness to spend much on more mundane necessities such as groceries and clothes. Even then, most couples are not fully aware of each other's stories and the way those stories evolved.

This is why we believe that it's imperative to have a full-disclosure money discussion. Use the written stories to explore your money relationships and how they translate into behaviors. If your spouse's parents were stingy with money, is his extravagance an act of rebellion or a way of overcompensating? If you grew up in a family in which no one ever talked about money, do you have a hard time talking to your kids about money issues?

When couples don't know each other's money stories, there are always surprises. Ellen, for instance, was recently surprised when Jesse insisted he needed to buy a wheelbarrow. A middle-aged couple—this was the second marriage for both of them—they bought a home at the beach with a small front yard and a wood deck with potted plants where a backyard would normally be found. One Saturday morning, Jesse said that he was off to the garden shop to buy a wheelbarrow. Ellen's response was, "Why do we need a wheelbarrow? We don't have a backyard, and the gardener takes care of the front. Save the money." "I want one," replied Jesse. "I used to have a wheelbarrow at my old house, and I can find a use for one here."

This was the start of a minor argument that could easily have escalated into a major one if Ellen and Jesse had not taken the time to talk about their money backgrounds. It turned out that Jesse's background had turned him into an acquirer of things and Ellen's had caused her to become a saver and recycler of things. Though this discussion didn't stop Jesse and Ellen from debating certain money issues, it did clear the air and prevent a major argument.

Money stories can be as strange and idiosyncratic as people themselves, and you should be willing to tell your story, warts and all, even if you're worried your spouse will find it odd. Paul and Debbie were married for eight years when an incident with a living room couch triggered the storytelling. The living room couch was the bane of Debbie's existence. It was a hand-me-down from her parents that Paul and Debbie were given when they were married. It had been recovered and sagged badly in the middle. At dinner one evening, Debbie announced that since the local furniture store was having a sale, the time had come to replace the living room couch. "But," Paul protested, "we can't just go buy a new couch; what would we do with the old one?" Paul's money story involved an attachment to anything that still functioned; he could not conceive of giving away something old if it still worked.

Ideally, couples will share their money stories early in their relationships, for their children's sake, if not for their own. Once couples know their money stories, they can start to grasp what money means to each of them and identify the emotional and psychological themes attached to their relationship with money. Understanding these themes helps them determine whether they are sending their kids the wrong messages about money in a wide variety of situations.

YOUR MONEY PERSONALITY

As you write your money story, you'll see that you have a particular relationship with money. It's important for every parent to understand the implications of this relationship, since it directly affects the messages you're sending your kids.

Just what do psychologists mean when they talk about a *personality*? A widely used definition developed by Theodore Millon defines personality as "a pattern of deeply embedded and broadly exhibited cognitive [how we think], affective [how we feel] and overt behavioral [how we behave] traits that persist over extended periods of time." So our money personality is how we think about money, how we feel about money and how we behave with money.

This personality gets expressed in three separate dimensions: the acquisition, the use and the management of money. To determine whether your money relationship in each dimension is normal, think of a twelve-inch ruler. The middle eight inches represent a secure relationship with money. The first two inches and the last two inches each represent different types of insecure relationships with money.

When we say that your money relationship in one of these three dimensions is normal or secure, two criteria are being met: (1) your relationship in that dimension will not get you into money trouble and (2) you are reasonably content with the relationship; you might want to be more organized or save a bit more or spend a little less or earn some more, but, all things considered, the situation is acceptable. When you have an insecure relationship in one of the money dimensions, either that relationship has already gotten you into money trouble or it may someday. With an insecure relationship, people often feel anxious or worried and sometimes view their money problems as inevitable. At the extreme ends of the ruler are people whose relationship with money is so abnormal that it can correctly be viewed as pathological: for example, someone who has an adequate to high income but loses his home because he doesn't pay his bills or goes to prison for tax evasion.

Each of us tends to have different degrees of security or insecurity when dealing with the three dimensions of acquisition, use and management of money. In addition, one or two of these dimensions tends to be more important to us than the others; one person may be more interested in saving while someone else is focused on management. There is nothing wrong or abnormal if one relationship is more important than the others. The mere fact that you are more focused on acquisition than use or management does not, by itself, imply that you have taken that relationship to an extreme.

Let's look at each area in more detail so that you can be aware of which relationship is most important to you and so that you can be conscious of whether your words and actions are insecure in any way; this will help you recognize any negative messages you might be sending to your kids.

Acquisition. Acquisition is the dimension that relates to how you get money. On one end of the ruler, you have the *avoidants,* who believe that money is the root of all evil. At the other end, you have the *insatiables*, who equate money with happiness and sometimes will break the law and bend the rules to acquire more. A wonderful example of an insatiable is John D. Rockefeller. At the time when he was the wealthiest man in the world, he was asked by a reporter, "How much money is enough?" His answer: "Just a little bit more." Most of us tend to be somewhere in the middle eight inches of the ruler; we neither fear money nor are prepared to break the law to acquire more.

Use. Use is the dimension of how you save or spend money. On one end of the spectrum you have the *miser*. Our favorite miser is Hetty Green. Hetty was born in 1834 into a wealthy New England family and inherited $7.5 million at age twenty-one. Through careful investing, she built her inheritance into a fortune. The October 1998 edition of *American Heritage* ranks Hetty as thirty-sixth out of the forty richest Americans in history. Expressed in today's dollars, her fortune had a buying power estimated at $17.3 billion. Yet Hetty's penny-pinching was truly pathological. In one infamous incident, her refusal to pay for medical care for her fifteen-year-old son resulted in the eventual amputation of his leg! At the other end of the ruler is the *compulsive overspender*. Again, most of us are in the middle, being reasonably careful and conscious of our use of money.

Management. Management is the dimension that describes everything from paying bills to managing your savings. As savings increase, some of these management functions are often delegated to professional advisers. On one end of the ruler you have the *obsessive-compulsive*, who micromanages down to the last dime. At the other end you have the *chaotic* individual who is extremely disorganized or procrastinates in paying bills to such an extent that his or her credit is often ruined.

The dividing lines between secure and insecure relationships are fuzzy. The difference between secure and insecure is a combination of emotion (are you content or anxious about the relationship?) and finance (will the relationship get you into money trouble?). Because the difference between secure and insecure is a complex, gray area, we may not be aware that our relationships with money are creating problems for our children. If, however, we focus on our behaviors in the areas of acquisition, use and management, we can gain the type of information that can help us control our negative behaviors. Therefore, try the following:

1. *Determine whether you acquire, use and manage money in ways that place you at the ends of our imaginary ruler. To make an accurate determination, don't rely only on your own assessment. Ask your spouse or anyone else close to you whether your behaviors fall in the normal or abnormal range. Use your money story to help make this determination.*

2. *If you conclude that you're in the abnormal range in any area, try to list specific things you've said or done that may have communicated a negative money message to your kids. For instance, if you determine that you are a compulsive overspender, you might list "Bought four model airplanes for my nine-year-old when we were at the store and he asked for just one."*

3. *Make a conscious effort to manage these types of behaviors. Your goal should not be to eliminate them entirely; that's not necessary. A more realistic goal is to reduce their frequency. One bout of overspending a year isn't going to hurt your child; doing it twenty times a year might.*

4. *Have your spouse go through this same exercise and then compare results. If you help each other manage your respective behaviors—if you can wave a yellow flag when your spouse falls into old, counterproductive money routines when your kids are around—you can lessen the likelihood that you're both telling your kids the wrong stories. It also will make you aware if you're telling your child one story ("Save every penny") and your spouse is telling another ("Life is short, so buy what you want"). Remember, though, correct-*

ing your spouse requires a certain amount of tact and diplomacy. Don't turn your correction into a criticism and spark a money fight.

When you understand your money personality, it helps your kids relate to money in each of these dimensions in healthy ways. When you have your story straight, you can send positive messages about acquisition, use and management, helping your children build their own internal structure for dealing with money issues. In acquisition, your kids learn that money makes a good servant but a bad master, in the words of the sixteenth-century English philosopher Francis Bacon. In the dimension of use, they develop a value system based on saving and spending appropriately as well as giving to those in need. In terms of management, you help them internalize the importance of intelligent financial management and record keeping, while avoiding going to extremes in either area.

If you're aware of your money personality, you're less likely to send your kids negative money messages. Still, there are messages in particular that we're all vulnerable to: money as taboo and money as cause of argument.

TABOOS AND ARGUMENTS

As a result of the society in which we live and the tensions involved in marriage, we can end up

- *treating money as a taboo topic; or*
- *teaching that money is the source of anxiety and arguments.*

Let's look at why these are such negative messages and what you can do to avoid sending them.

Money as a Taboo Topic

Psychologists and financial writers love referring to money as the last taboo. In 1913, Freud commented in *On Beginning the Treatment* that money questions are treated "in the same manner as sexual matters, with the same inconsistency, prudishness and hypocrisy." Today, everyone seems to be talking to their kids about sex: A search for *children* and *sex education* on Amazon.com produced 4,667 hits. Talking to kids about money still seems to be the exception for many of us; a similar search on Amazon.com for *children* and *financial education* produced only 267 hits, with most of them being books that referred to children but did not deal with childhood financial education.

We don't talk to our children about money because we don't know what to say. Our own parents didn't talk to us about money, and their parents didn't talk to them about money. Given this multigenerational silence, it's no wonder that the topic is off-limits. We may not consciously consider it taboo, but unconsciously, we avoid talking about such things as our salaries, the importance of saving, conspicuous consumption and other topics. We may also make excuses to ourselves or our kids about why we don't talk about money. Saying that it's crass to discuss such a subject is a common excuse. In reality, we lack the language and framework necessary to have a good discussion.

When we don't know how to talk to our kids about money, we can't handle the natural curiosity that arises in the initiative stage of development. Instead of satisfying their curiosity and making them feel comfortable with the topic, we turn it into a secret. Typically, parents respond to money questions from kids in pat phrases that simply stop the conservation. The most reliable money conversation stopper is "We can't afford it" or some variation, such as "I don't have the money."

There is nothing wrong with using these conversation stoppers if you really can't afford it. The real problem arises when you can afford it, you say you can't and your actions demonstrate that you're lying. For example, Mom tells her daughter that they can't afford a newly released animated video prominently displayed next to the checkout stand. She tells her this as they are unloading their shopping cart filled to the brim with such things as premium hair conditioners and other expensive items. Then her daughter watches Mom pull out a credit card and pay for everything.

What messages was Mom sending when she dismissed her daughter's request for the video with "We can't afford it"? One message was that Mom wouldn't always tell her the truth, since she was obviously fibbing about not being able to afford the video. Even at five, her daughter could figure out that if Mom could pay for all the other stuff, she probably could have afforded the video. Another message was that the daughter's wishes were much less important than Mom's. A third message: If you don't have money or can't afford something, use a credit card to pay for things. The overarching message, though, was that money is not a suitable topic for discussion. The "I can't afford it" was dismissive. Mom was conveying to her daughter that this was not something up for discussion, reinforcing the taboo aspect of money.

What should Mom have said or done? For most parents, "I can't afford it" translates to "I don't want to buy that for you" without having to explain their reasons. Unfortunately, using "I can't afford it" this way combines lying to your child with passing up a wonderful opportunity to share your values. As parents, we often keep our values in our head and don't explain them to our children. Maybe it's a plastic action figure that you don't want to buy because you think it is overpriced junk, or maybe it's a pair of $275 aviator sunglasses that you consider too expensive for a twelve-year-old who lost his last two pairs of $8 sunglasses. Or maybe it is simply the third time today that your child has asked you to buy him something and you feel he is being greedy. Therefore, view these situations as teachable moments and use them to convey your values. Tell your child, "It's overpriced," or "I don't want to buy it because it's poorly made," or "The company that makes it exploits child labor," or "You have enough action figures; I don't want to buy you any more." If your child is interested, engage him in a discussion of the reasons behind your statement. Depending on his age, you can talk about everything from diminishing natural resources to an overly materialistic society. You can relate your own experiences growing up and how they shaped your beliefs about morality, quality and the like. The key, though, is to treat money as a subject worthy of discussion.

During an interview on National Public Radio, the moderator, Larry Mantle, told us a story of growing up in the sixties. Larry saw a James Bond briefcase advertised on television and couldn't live without one. His father explained that he wasn't going to buy him one, but he didn't stop there. Instead, they drove to a local toy store, where Larry had the opportunity to inspect the briefcase and discover that it was, in his words, "overpriced junk" that looked nothing like the one on television. To this day, he values the lesson he learned by having *no* accompanied by an explanation.

Money as a Source of Anxiety and Arguments

You'll find that we keep returning to the topic of money fights in this book, but there's a good reason for this. Money arguments are a recurring theme in just about every marriage—and certainly among many divorced parents. They're tricky to prevent, though, because they often are a reflexive response of your money personality. Therefore, we want to look at these fights from a number of angles. Here, let's examine how they become part of the money story parents tell kids and the accompanying anxiety they often produce in children.

At the Gallo Institute, we have worked with some of the wealthiest families in America as well as many middle-class couples, and we can tell you that money fights are not a function of how much money you have. One couple might fight over whether their third vacation of the year should be to Spain or Japan, while another couple might fight over whether they can even afford to take a week off for a vacation.

The list of money topics couples fight over could fill this book; here is a much shorter version of the list:

- *how much to spend on the purchase of a house*
- *the obsessive-compulsiveness of one spouse regarding finances*
- *risky investment decisions*
- *what you feel is the outlandish cost of a child's toy*
- *public or private education (a state college versus a private one)*
- *the amount of money spent on clothes*
- *whether one spouse should be a stay-at-home parent and give up his or her job*
- *the decision to look for a better-paying job (and leave a lower-paying one that the individual loves)*
- *the need to buy a bigger house (or a house in a more upscale community with better schools)*
- *where all the money goes (and the bad record keeping that results in this argument)*
- *where all the money goes (because one spouse kept good records and used the records to blame his or her spouse)*

While the types of fights vary, the underlying reason for the fights is the same: Husbands and wives learned different money scripts as children, and the differences create tension when money issues arise. They naturally assume that their spouses will be following the same script and are shocked and saddened to discover that their spouse's script is very different from their own.

Linda and Charlie had been married for fourteen years when they realized they needed help. They had been arguing about their eleven-year-old son's allowance for weeks, placing a strain on their marriage. Ken was receiving five dollars a week, and he kept running out of allowance before he ran out of week. To help him learn to manage his allowance better, Charlie told Ken to keep a ledger to track how he was spending his money, but Ken wasn't keeping the ledger up-to-date. Charlie wanted to reduce Ken's allowance by a dollar a week each time the ledger didn't balance. Linda didn't think it was such a big deal and felt that the penalty was ridiculously harsh.

In fourteen years of marriage, Linda and Charlie rarely talked about their money stories with each other. When they finally did start sharing their stories, they began to understand and appreciate their differences. As a child, Linda had received a regular allowance from her parents, and she viewed allowances as a valuable tool to help her kids learn to manage money and make choices. Charlie, on the other hand, grew up in a family that couldn't afford to give him an allowance, and he valued self-sufficiency. Their fight, therefore, wasn't really about Ken's spending habits or his failure to keep the ledger up-to-date; it was about competing values they had learned as children and expected their spouse to share. When Linda and Charlie saw their fight for what it really was, they realized that not only was their argument confusing Ken, but they were missing an opportunity to help Ken learn a positive money lesson by taking money away as a punishment. They told Ken that they would help him with the ledger, and if an accurate ledger showed that his allowance wasn't sufficient, they would be willing to discuss a reasonable increase.

If you fight with your spouse about money, it may be that the two of you are reading from different scripts based on different values you learned as children. Your fight is really over the psychological issues and the values that are hiding behind the financial issues. Another example is provided by Janice and Frank. Janice grew up in a home in which her father worked and controlled how the money was spent. Mom stayed home and acquiesced to Dad's decisions. As a result, she learned that money determines who has the power and control in the family. The role of the spouse with less money is to agree with the decisions reached by the other spouse. All of this added up to her money script, a series of expectations about how a husband and wife carry out their roles when it comes to money. When Janice married Frank, she carried this script into the marriage and expected Frank to be reading from the same script. But Frank grew up in a family where his parents shared financial decision-making responsibility. Janice felt that Frank wanted her to take on financial duties that were his job, and Frank complained that Janice wouldn't participate in making important family decisions.

As we noted earlier, some spouses keep a secret stash of money for particular types of purchases. Sometimes, their motivation for these stashes is to avoid money fights, other times to retain a sense of autonomy and security. No matter what the reason for the secrecy, the result is often a huge blowup when the hidden-money behavior comes to light, with feelings of betrayal in one spouse and guilt in the other. For the children who witness the emergence of these feelings as well as the gargantuan, secret-ending fight, not only does money become associated with a source of conflict, anger, guilt and betrayal, but it feeds the concept of money as a taboo subject.

To avoid these secrecy fights, we recommend a Money Amnesty Day. Set aside a time for you and your spouse to sit down and reveal any money secrets that you may have been keeping from each other. Agree in advance that you will forgive whatever is revealed so long as the behavior stops.

Of course, these amnesty days aren't going to end all money fights. If you and your spouse grew up with different money values, some tension is always going to exist between you. What you need to resolve is to keep this tension from erupting into armed combat; even fighting in private can hurt children, since they often can read their parents and know when and about what they've been fighting without actually witnessing the bout. Getting your money stories straight means resolving to limit your fights to infrequent skirmishes.

Financially intelligent parents present a unified front when dealing with money issues. This behavior takes a bit of work and practice, and we've found that a number of techniques facilitate integrating this behavior into your routine.

TOOLS, TIPS AND TECHNIQUES: HOW TO COMMUNICATE A CONSISTENT, POSITIVE MESSAGE

Perhaps the first and best thing you and your spouse can do is to create three basic money messages that will guide what the two of you say and do with your kids for everything from allowances to buying toys to saving money. You should agree on money messages for acquisition, use and management. These basic money messages serve as scripts you can use again and again in a consistent manner when dealing with money issues. Obviously, your messages should reflect the values you and your spouse agree on, but here is a sample of three that you can adopt or adapt:

Acquisition. Setting an ambitious financial goal is fine as long as you don't become consumed, obsessed and otherwise a slave to this goal.

Use. Money can be used to buy both necessities and luxuries, but not to buy things to impress others or to establish your own worth.

Management. Keeping track of finances is responsible behavior, but to keep track of them down to the last penny or to spend hours record keeping every night may involve shirking your responsibility to family and friends and other more meaningful pursuits.

A good place to start is for you and your spouse to write down your version of the three messages. Then trade lists. Agree in advance that you will compromise if your money messages are in conflict. Compromise requires that you listen to your spouse and abandon black-and-white thinking in which "I'm willing to listen to you, but I'm right and you're wrong." Remember that the question isn't who's right and who's wrong; it's how the basic money messages you are jointly creating are going to affect the emotional well-being of your child! Black-and-white thinking gets in the way of the give-and-take necessary for good compromises. Try to understand your spouse's position and respond constructively with the best interests of your child in mind. Responding to your husband's proposals by telling him that he is as irresponsible with money as his mother is does not make for good compromises! Watch your body language. Rolling your eyes or sighing loudly suggests that your spouse's position is worthless.

Even after you both agree on the three basic money messages, your childhood values will still have a powerful influence on your behaviors, making conflict possible. Once again, compromise must come into play. Your spouse wants to give your daughter a car on her sixteenth birthday. You are opposed. When the two of you disagree over a money issue, you need to ask yourselves whether the way you are looking at the issue is based on fear or love. You may fear that buying your teenage daughter a car on her sixteenth birthday will spoil her forever. Your spouse may fear that the neighbors will think you are tightwads if you don't give her the car. Fear makes compromise difficult. Looking at the issue based on love means asking what is in the best interests of your daughter. It's much easier to reach an agreement when you approach the issue with your child's best interests in mind.

We also recommend that couples try to share financial responsibilities. Divide financial chores based on your talents and interests. One spouse may be better at dealing with mistakes on bills, like not getting credit for returned merchandise, while the other might be better at securing bids to have the bathroom painted. The spouse who makes more money than the other should not receive the lion's share of responsibility. Just because you make more money than your partner doesn't mean you're a better money manager. In fact, we know families in which the breadwinners are so focused on work that they lack the time and energy for money-management responsibilities. Sharing these responsibilities sends kids the message that money management is something both Mom and Dad—and more specifically, women and men—are equally capable of handling.

Finally, don't be cavalier or unthinking about your money-related decisions and actions. We realize that you can't be hyperaware of every money decision—you can't stop and analyze each request your child makes for a toy and how your answer dovetails with your values—but you can regularly evaluate whether your money words and deeds are consistent and clear. Specifically,

- *Are you and your spouse saying and doing things regarding allowances, gifts and so on that communicate the same message or that send opposing messages?*
- *Are you avoiding major money battles, both in front of your children and in private?*
- *Are you talking to your spouse about money issues that arise and formulating a plan to handle these issues in keeping with your agreed-upon values?*

Keeping these questions in mind will help you keep your money stories straight.

Answer to Financially Intelligent Brainteaser

The correct answer is C. Compromise and calm discussion will communicate to your kids that being flexible about financial issues is a good policy and that difficult decisions can be resolved without hostility and without one parent making an arbitrary pronouncement. Public or private financial fighting will have a negative impact on kids, and you should do everything possible to limit their exposure to these arguments. Refusing to discuss the issue may avoid exposing them to a fight, but it also sends the message that ignoring important financial subjects is a viable option. ◆

6

FACILITATE FINANCIAL REFLECTION: HELPING YOUR CHILDREN LEARN TO MAKE GOOD MONEY CHOICES

Financially Intelligent Brainteaser

Your eccentric aunt Martha dies, and she has left your twelve-year-old son five thousand dollars in her will. When you inform him of this fact, he is tremendously excited. He starts listing all the things he wants to buy with the money: fifteen video games, a new computer with enhanced game-playing capacity, a flat-screen television for his bedroom and on and on. Your son asks how soon he'll receive the money and whether he can get all of it in cash; his intention is clearly to spend it the moment he gets it. How might you respond so that he reflects on his good fortune and the ways it might be used?

A. Make him feel guilty about being so materialistic; tell him he should think about all the kids in the world who don't have enough money to buy food, let alone video games.
B. Tell him that the money is going into his college fund and explain to him the long-term benefits of saving the money rather than spending it immediately.
C. Ask him whether he thinks Aunt Martha's intention was for him to spend the entire five thousand dollars on electronic toys.
D. Tell him he can spend 5 percent of the money on anything he wants, but that he must also give 5 percent to the Society for the Prevention of Cruelty to Winged Creatures, Aunt Martha's favorite charity.

(Answer at end of chapter)

When it comes to making money decisions, kids are frequently impulsive. In fact, when it comes to making most decisions, kids are impulsive. It doesn't matter whether the choice involves money, food or friends; kids often react without thinking. Children simply aren't born with the capacity for self-observation and the ability to control their impulses and make decisions based on weighing alternatives. As financially intelligent parents, we need to teach our children how to think in terms of alternatives before they spend all their lemonade money on a video game or, when they're older, on the roulette wheel in Las Vegas instead of a house for their own family. Jumping from lemonade money to gambling money is not a big jump from a psychological perspective.

Thinking in terms of alternatives is called *reflective thinking*. Learning how to reflect before making a decision is a great life skill and the hallmark of people who make good choices in everything from careers to relationships and from purchases to investments. Being able to reflect after you make a decision and learning from the consequences is another crucial life lesson. In *The Secure Child*, Stanley Greenspan, MD, observes that there are dozens of opportunities to engage your child in reflective thinking every day. Greenspan describes the process of helping boys and girls develop the tools they need to engage in self-reflection as a gift, one that will enable them to become responsible citizens.

Unlike some of the other money behaviors we're suggesting you adopt, facilitating financial reflection may seem less compelling on the surface. If you look below the surface, however, you'll understand how crucial reflection is in a child's development.

THE MARSHMALLOW TEST

You might not connect marshmallows with the benefits of self-reflection, but a great deal of what we know about kids and impulse control stems from a 1960s experiment with marshmallows. Psychologist Walter Mischel developed a test of emotional self-control that involved offering marshmallows to the four-year-old children of Stanford professors, graduate students and employees. The kids were brought into a room at Stanford one by one and given a marshmallow. They were told they could eat it then, but if they could wait for about twenty minutes, until the researcher returned from a pretend errand, they would receive two marshmallows. Researchers observed the children through a one-way mirror. Some of them were able to wait the twenty minutes until the researcher returned and then received their second marshmallow. They found ways to divert themselves from thinking about the marshmallow: some covered their eyes so they wouldn't have to see the treat; others rested their head in their arms, played games with their hands, sang songs or even tried to take a nap. Others consumed the marshmallow as soon as the researcher left the room.

Fourteen years later, the kids were interviewed. The results were dramatic: the kids who were able to wait for the second marshmallow were, as eighteen-year-olds, more socially competent, less likely to go to pieces under stress, better able to deal with challenges and more self-reliant, and on average, they scored 210 points higher on their SAT tests than those who were unable to delay gratification!

Why were some of the four-year-olds able to figure out that it was in their best interest to delay gratification while others were not? And why did learning self-control at age four have such a dramatic effect on their lives as adolescents? The answer, in a word, is reflection. Parents taught the two-marshmallow kids to reflect on their feelings in terms of choices ("I can have one now, but I can have two later"), values ("I prioritize long-term gain over short-term satisfaction") and consequences ("I will satisfy my hunger better if I wait versus satisfying it temporarily if I eat one immediately"). These lessons last throughout the child's life.

We have found that financially intelligent parents teach their children to evaluate all their options rather than make impulsive decisions. As a result, these children acquire the skills to make good choices. Like the four-year-olds who were able to resist eating the marshmallow immediately, kids need to understand that, when it comes to money, there are things to do other than spend it immediately—they can save it, they can invest it or they can give it to charity—and each has certain results. Stanley Greenspan has observed that children who develop the ability to engage in self-reflection and think in terms of choices and consequences grow into teenagers who "can solve problems and assess and evaluate their own impulses and desires." Teenagers without this ability to engage in self-reflection are "limited to their immediate and often impulsive reactions to events."

You can model reflective behavior in many ways—your decisions about careers, ethical matters and so on—but your money behaviors have a tremendous impact on children. From the time they're little, kids pay attention to how you determine the amount of an allowance, whether to buy a bigger house, and how to choose between a luxurious family vacation and putting money away for a son's or daughter's tuba lessons. If you exhibit reflective behavior, it provides a model not just for your child's own money behaviors but for how she acts in all areas of her life.

REFLECTING ON WHAT REFLECTION MEANS

Let's take a moment to examine what reflection really entails. Your children learn to make choices by thinking reflectively. When a person thinks reflectively, she is examining her thoughts, emotions, ideas and beliefs before she acts. In other words, engaging in reflective thinking is having a conversation with yourself. Reflective thinking after you act is just as important as reflecting before you act, especially when you've made a mistake. You want to ask yourself such questions as "Why did I do that?" and "Do I feel good about what I did?" James Joyce described mistakes as "the portal to opportunity." He meant that reflecting on mistakes allows you to learn from failure and generate fresh opportunities. Kids learn valuable lessons by doing something impulsively, reflecting on why they did it, and resolving not to repeat the same mistake.

Our kids acquire the ability to think reflectively by observing how we act when we are making choices and by having us engage them in reflective dialogues. Reflective dialogues are conversations we have with our children that deal not only with their behavior but also with their mental states and with choices and alternatives. They are true conversations, not lectures. In a reflective discussion, you don't simply respond yes or no to your child's questions or comments. Instead, you ask what, when, why and how to help them form an opinion and reflect on their own wishes and ideas; this is the foundation of abstract thinking.

If you have young kids, facilitate these discussions by getting down on the floor with them. Set aside perhaps twenty to thirty minutes every day for floor time. Turn off the television and turn on the answering machine. Being at your kid's level, eye to eye, generates a sense of equality. During floor time, your child owns you. Do whatever your child wants to do, even if it means playing the same game for the zillionth time. There should be no rules except no hurting people and no breaking toys. Let your child set the emotional tone of the play, and follow his lead. As you talk and play and interact, you are establishing an environment in which your child feels comfortable talking about anything. This means that you can ask questions that allow your child to explore his mind and to think about alternatives. You will be amazed at the dozens of opportunities for reflective thinking that arise. For instance, you are reading "Little Red Riding Hood" to your five-year-old. Ask him what would have happened if Little Red Riding Hood had gone straight to Grandmother's house and had not stopped to pick flowers.

Stimulating financial reflection during these times is relatively easy, but you need to employ different methods with children of different ages. With very small children, you can read fairy tales or make up ones of your own devised to get them thinking about money choices. "The Midas Touch" and "Rumpelstilskin" are two examples of fairy tales that revolve around money issues. Ask your child a question such as, "If you were able to turn everything into gold with a touch of your finger, how might you use that power to do good?"

With kids a bit older, you might play board games such as Monopoly that involve financial transactions. After the game is over, ask them what they thought the turning point of the game was that caused them to win or lose. With hindsight, what might they have done differently? If the game had been real life, what might they have done differently, and why?

With some preteens and adolescents, you probably don't need the prop of a story or a game. Instead, you can capitalize on the common money issues in their lives to prompt financial reflection. Suppose they decide to spend a fifty-dollar birthday gift from Grandpa on CDs. You might ask whether they would have spent the entire gift on CDs if Grandpa had given them one hundred dollars. Too often, parents prematurely cut off reflective discussions with yes or no answers: "Yes, you can have the money to buy the bike," or "No, I'm not going to spend money for you to go listen to that awful rock group perform." As difficult as it is to get teenagers to think and talk about certain subjects with you, money topics generally intrigue adolescents. Before saying yes or no, throw out some questions that will cause your children to consider why they want to make a specific purchase or what other choices they might have, given the money that is available, or other ways they might achieve their objectives.

Once your child has a driver's license and wants to borrow the car, don't just say yes or no every time she asks. Instead, occasionally ask where she wants to go, whether her homework is done and whether there is anything else she wants to accomplish today. Asking your child these types of questions helps further reflection.

If you have difficulty engaging your teenager in this type of discussion—you may be dealing with a sullen or frequently silent teen—increase the hanging-out time you spend with him. This is the equivalent of floor time, in that you leave your parent agenda behind and give your child your undivided attention. Hanging out means taking your child to a favorite restaurant or a concert or sporting event; it means taking him shopping at the mall or for a hike in the woods. Just being with him in a fresh environment gives him the opportunity to talk about issues in his life—many times, these issues relate to money. For instance:

- *Your son wants to buy his girlfriend a particular present but doesn't know whether his girlfriend will like it, and it costs a lot of money.*
- *Your daughter is thinking about taking a part-time job after school but isn't sure whether it's a good idea.*
- *Your son wants to save money to buy a guitar or go on a school-sponsored trip, but he's not sure of the best way to go about it.*
- *Your daughter is worried because you and your spouse just got divorced and she knows the divorce has created financial tensions.*

Whatever the issue might be, don't automatically respond with a solution. Ask your child what alternatives he has thought about. When you have a reflective dialogue with your child, stay away from being judgmental. Nothing turns off your child faster than a lecture masquerading as a conversation. You want to help your child learn the process of being reflective so that he can learn to make his own judgments.

Finally, recognize that it's natural for teenagers to dream about being wealthy and that you can use this fantasy to initiate reflective dialogues. Our friend and colleague Dr. Stephan Poulter has included a "million-dollar money game" in his book *Father Your Son: How to Become the Father You've Always Wanted to Be,* which you can use with your teenager. During hanging out time, ask your child the following questions:

- *If I were to write you a check for a million dollars, what would you do with the money?*
- *Would you spend all the money, or would you save any of it?*

- *Would you think about giving any of it to charity? If so, which charities and why?*
- *If you had a million dollars, do you think all your problems would be solved? What problems might you still have despite the money? What new problems might you develop because of all that money?*
- *If you had a million dollars, how do you think your friends would treat you? Do you think it would be hard to tell who were your real friends and which people were just sucking up to you because you were rich?*

Whenever you engage your child in reflective dialogue, don't just listen to what he says. Offer opinions and discuss what you might do as well. You are a role model, a touchstone for your child. Your opinions can help him decide where to draw the line between acceptable and unacceptable behavior as he evaluates options and their possible consequences.

MODEL REFLECTIVE BEHAVIOR

As important as it is to ask questions and stimulate discussions designed to encourage reflective financial behaviors in your children, you also need to be reflective yourself. Many parents don't practice what they preach, at least when their kids are watching. To assess how reflective you are, answer the following questions:

- *When you buy a big-ticket item such as a car or a computer, do you talk about the purchase with your spouse and do a lot of research before you make the purchase?*
- *Are you likely to comparison shop before making a buying decision?*

- *Do you usually give curt, immediate yes or no answers when your child asks you a money-related question?*

- *Are you the type of person who thinks before acting when it comes to significant financial decisions such as investments, buying a home and so on?*

- *When you're sharing a story with your child about your difficult decisions regarding careers (e.g., trade-offs involving better salary, lower job satisfaction), lifestyle (choosing to live in a given home or community) and money policies (choosing to save for a summer vacation rather than buying an expensive new television), do you also share how you struggled with the decisions?*

- *Has your child ever encountered you just sitting and thinking about something; not reading, not watching, not listening, but just pondering a significant issue?*

No one is always reflective, and that should not be your goal. At the same time, you should not hide how much thought and self-questioning go into your decision making, especially regarding money issues. If you are impulsive when it comes to money issues (and other issues as well), you should make an effort to moderate that impulsiveness.

Many parents don't realize that they unconsciously hide their decision-making process from their kids under the mistaken belief that they won't understand or they'll think Mom and Dad are weak and indecisive. They make decisions involving emotions, money and values without explaining to their children all the factors that helped them arrive at the choices they made. For instance, we were standing in front of a flower stall at a local farmers' market one Sunday morning when we overheard a conversation about money and values between a young mother and her six-year-old son. The mother examined some flowers, put them back and said to her son: "Let's buy our flowers at the other stand. The man wraps them very nicely for us, *and loyalty is important.*" In two brief sentences, this mother quickly and clearly communicated to her son what she valued and why she was making a particular purchasing decision. Not only did her son learn an important lesson about values as they relate to spending, but he also learned about reflective thinking. Specifically, he discovered that thinking about loyalty helps make a good purchasing choice. He also found out that if you set out to purchase something, you don't have to purchase it from the first seller you encounter. Instead, you should consider options, such as price, quality or, in this case, your relationship with different sellers.

REFLECTIVE DIALOGUE TIPS AND TECHNIQUES

You may find yourself frustrated as you attempt to put this money behavior into practice, especially with adolescents. When it comes to one particular money dimension—use—teens can act like they don't have a brain in their heads. Convincing them that it's a good idea to stop, ponder and reponder a decision is difficult, especially if you're trying to create this particular behavior later rather than earlier in your child's life. If you're encountering difficulty, try waiting until the consequences of a bad purchase really sink in before initiating a reflective dialogue.

When our youngest son was fourteen, we gave him a clothing allowance. He was overjoyed at the freedom he suddenly had and announced that the first thing he was going to buy was a long, black wool overcoat he had been admiring. We gently reminded him that fall and winter temperatures were mild in Southern California and that spring and summer temperatures averaged in the eighties and nineties. Perhaps, we suggested, it wasn't a good idea to spend 50 percent of his clothing budget for the semester on an overcoat! Our son was unmoved and soon became the proud owner of the overcoat he always wanted. During that winter, it was cold enough for him to wear the coat twice. We avoided the temptation to lecture him about wasting his money and the importance of impulse control. Instead, we waited until the coat had hung in the closet for several months and only then asked him what he thought about his decision to buy the overcoat. He contemplated our question and responded that he really liked the coat but he guessed that it had taught him to think longer before spending money. It was nice to have the coat, he explained, but he couldn't wear it very often and he didn't have enough money left over to buy some of the clothes he now wished he had purchased instead.

As parents, we often jump the gun and lecture our children about their impulsive behaviors rather than biding our time and waiting until the consequences of these behaviors dawn on them. Lecturing kids about how they are spending their money is a fruitless exercise; they may appear to be listening, but their brain is in sleep mode. Reflective dialogue, however, usually gets through to them. By asking questions at appropriate times, we help them reflect on their past money behaviors. They become actively involved in thinking about the consequences of that behavior—"I spent too much on the overcoat and didn't have enough to buy other clothes I wanted later during the semester"—as well as the alternatives. If enough time passes and they move past their initial defensiveness, they usually tell themselves things like, "I could have bought a cheaper overcoat or not bought one at all since it was too warm most of the time to wear it, and I would have had money to buy the other clothes I wanted."

Give your child enough time and space so that you can practice this money behavior effectively. Consider, too, that some children are unable or unwilling to learn from their experiences, repeating the same mistakes ad infinitum. Kids who don't learn from experience are usually those who have not been exposed to a sufficient amount of reflective dialogue.

We would also recommend you employ the Family Money Diary to involve your children in reflective dialogues. To create a money diary, take a piece of paper and create six columns. Label them as follows:

Purchase	Cost	Glad We Bought It	Disappointed We Bought It	Alone or with Others	Money Value

List the purchases you make. Check whether you are glad or disappointed about the purchase. Indicate whether you made the purchase on your own, whether you spoke to others about their experiences with the same or similar products and whether the purchase was a family project. In the sixth column, list the money values represented by the purchase. If you purchased the items on sale, a money value might be frugality. On the other hand, if you are disappointed in the purchase because the items turned out to be shoddily made, you might want to list the money value that you learned from the purchase—prudence might be an appropriate one in this instance.

Eric and Jenna have two children: a daughter, Monica, age eight, and a son, Nicholas, age ten. They used the Family Money Diary as a family project when it became apparent that Jenna needed a new car. As Monica and Nicholas got more involved in after-school sports, Jenna often found herself spending afternoons chauffeuring three or four kids and all of their equipment to games. Unfortunately, Jenna's midsize Chevy lacked both the seating and the storage space that soccer moms need. The obvious solution was to trade the Chevy in for something larger, but should it be a full-size car, a minivan, or an SUV? What make? What options? Rather than making these decisions themselves, Eric and Jenna decided to create a Family Money Diary and use the process of selecting the new car as an opportunity to help their kids engage in reflective thinking. They began by calling a family meeting and explaining the issue: Mom's car is too small, we need something larger and the two of you are going to help us select the new car! The kids were excited and began offering suggestions based on television commercials and the cars their friends' parents drove. In fact, they were ready to leave and buy the new car immediately.

"Not so fast," was Jenna's reply. Eric added, "We need to know what choices we have and then figure out what make and model is the best for us." Eric and Jenna explained that there were dozens of makes and models to choose from and that they needed to go about making their selection in a thoughtful way. The first step was to figure out what information they needed to know about each car. They handed out pencils and paper, and all four began to brainstorm the various categories of information they should obtain. Monica said that it was important to know how many people could sit in the car. Nicholas added that they needed to know how much cargo space it had. Jenna and Eric added such things as safety equipment, gas mileage, price, recall history and repair history from the *Consumer Reports* annual car issue. It took about fifteen minutes, and they had a list of about ten things they wanted to know about each car. Monica and Nicholas were assigned the job of getting some of this information from the Internet sites of the various manufacturers. Eric and Jenna would get the rest. Once they had all the information they were looking for, the family had a second meeting to decide on which vehicles they should test-drive. One was too expensive; one had a really bad repair record; one wouldn't carry enough people; one didn't have enough cargo space. They eliminated all but six SUVs and minivans. The test-drives narrowed the choice to two minivans that everyone agreed would be fine, and Eric and Jenna made the final decision based on trade-in and financing considerations, explaining to Monica and Nicholas how they made that decision.

The next step was to fill out the Family Money Diary. They all agreed that they were pleased with the purchase and that it represented the money value of educated buying. The entry looked like this:

Purchase	Cost	Glad We Bought It	Disappointed We Bought It	Alone or with Others	Money Value
Minivan	$28,000	Yes		Family Project	Educated Buying

If you use the money diary selectively, you can engage your children in the type of research, questioning and thinking that will turn reflection into a reflex. Obviously, you don't want to overuse this device so that it feels like a chore; you don't want your children to roll their eyes and say, "Here comes that money diary again." If you confine its use to major purchases, though, it should be an effective tool. You might also print up some money diary forms for your kids to use by themselves. Though they probably won't use them religiously, they might fill out a form on occasion when they're facing a difficult spending choice. As great as it is when kids engage in reflective dialogues with parents, they need to be able to have reflective dialogues with themselves.

Finally, we'd like to leave you with three additional ways you can encourage reflection when you talk to your kids about money issues.

Make a Conscious and Concerted Effort to Listen. This may seem obvious, but when your eight-year-old goes off on a seemingly endless monologue about the price of one type of baseball trading card versus another, you may find yourself zoning out. The human brain is capable of processing verbal information at a rate of 300 to 500 words a minute, but children tend to speak at a rate of no more than 200 to 250 words a minute. Younger children speak even more slowly. If your child is groping for the right word or slowly trying to put his feelings into words, you may start thinking about some problem from work instead of really listening, or you may interrupt him and finish his thought for him. In these instances, you're sending your child a message that what he's saying isn't that important. As a result, he may not attach enough importance to it so that he makes the effort to reflect. When you're really listening, on the other hand, you're motivating him to take his words—and his decisions—seriously.

Translate Your Child's Words into Their Underlying Meaning. Children can't always articulate their real money issues and the choices with which they're struggling. Even teenagers may be unable or unwilling to present their dilemmas clearly. As a result, you may miss a great opportunity to engage in a reflective dialogue—you falsely assume she's bringing up a trivial matter or one that doesn't require a conversation. Therefore, take a moment to consider what your child might really be talking about when she raises a money issue. For instance, five-year-old Janet came home from preschool and asked, "Mommy, do we have a million dollars?" Fortunately, Janet's mother was savvy about reflective dialogues, and instead of answering yes or no asked a question of her own: "Why are you asking?" It turned out that one of Janet's classmates had seen some homeless people at the local park and that a fellow five-year-old had asserted that one needed a million dollars to avoid becoming homeless. When it came to financial issues, Janet didn't know the difference between a million dollars and her elbow. She was really asking to be reassured that she was safe and wouldn't have to live on the street. Janet's mom explained to her the difference between their financial situation and that of a homeless person, giving her plenty upon which to reflect.

Clear the Roadblock of Unresolved Money Issues from Your Childhood. You may have the best of intentions but the worst of results. If you're trying and failing to stimulate the type of conversations we've addressed here, you may be unconsciously sabotaging your efforts. To have a conversation with your child in which he thinks about his choices and questions his decisions requires you to be in touch with your own issues. We know too many parents who ignore their kids when they should be encouraging them to talk, or who deliver lectures when they should listen. Frequently, kids bring up subjects that rub salt in a parent's childhood wounds, and parents respond to what happened in the past rather than what is taking place in the present. For instance, Jeff grew up in a home where his parents constantly fought over money. His father accused his mother of being a spendthrift who was going to send all of them to the poorhouse and his mother called his father an unreasonable tightwad. Whenever Jeff had to talk to his kids about money, he would be flooded with memories of his parents' fights and become tense and angry; while he wanted to say things that would help his kids be more reflective, the conversations would quickly deteriorate into accusations and lectures.

If you have unresolved issues, try to make yourself aware of the typical ways you sabotage conversations with your child. Like Jeff, perhaps you resort to accusations and lectures. Like other parents, you might finish your child's sentences and not give her the chance to express herself. Making an effort to catch yourself doing these things may help you manage these behaviors so that you and your child can engage in reflective dialogues. It's also possible that your issues are deep-seated, and in this instance, you might consider seeking professional counseling to deal with them.

Ultimately, these three suggestions as well as the other tools and techniques detailed in this chapter are designed to jump-start your child's reflective engine. The dialogues are simply a precursor to your child's engaging in this type of behavior on his own. Guiding your child in a reflective direction from an early age can help him think before he buys and use his money in ways that are in keeping with his values. Perhaps even more significantly, financial reflection can naturally encourage your child to be reflective about a wide variety of events in his life. Money issues offer opportunities to teach kids broader life skills. Ideally, once your child practices reflection in the financial arena, he will reflect before he starts smoking, drinking, ignoring schoolwork or engaging in other tempting teenage behaviors. As adults, people who are wise, happy and self-fulfilled tend to be those who are routinely reflective. It is a great legacy to pass on to your children, and you can start with reflective money dialogues.

Answer to Financially Intelligent Brainteaser

The correct answer is C. Provocative questions are a great way to stimulate reflection. Asking your son to speculate on Aunt Martha's wishes for the money is a way to get him to think seriously rather than frivolously about the money. No doubt, he will ask himself whether Aunt Martha would be pleased if he spent all the money on electronic entertainment; he might also ask himself about what type of person Aunt Martha was, why she left him the money and what might be a more appropriate use of it. In terms of the other answers, A, making him feel guilty may cause him to beat himself up but not reflect on his choices. The other two possible responses, B and D, suggest that you should tell your son what to do with the money, but by providing definitive instructions, you leave him no room to reflect on other options. ◆

7

THE IMPORTANCE OF BEING A CHARITABLE FAMILY: GIVING BACK TO THE COMMUNITY

Financially Intelligent Brainteaser

You are the parent of a twelve-year-old boy and a fifteen-year-old girl, and you're concerned about their materialism. Though they're good kids at heart, they are always asking you and your spouse to buy them things—your son has a huge collection of computer games and your daughter loves brand-name clothes. You decide that volunteering will help them understand the larger world and recognize that there is more to life than can be found in things. You investigate a number of volunteer options.

Which of the following makes the most sense for your kids?

A. Have the family spend the summer in Costa Rica building homes for the homeless, living in tents and primitive conditions as do the people you're building homes for.

B. Insist that your children find a good cause that they believe in, justify why they believe it is a good cause and donate two dollars a week to it.

C. Take advantage of a school-sponsored program for kids and their parents to help paint, clean and raise money for another school in a poorer section of town.

D. Sign up yourself, your spouse and your kids for a walkathon designed to raise money for a disease your daughter's friend is suffering from.

(Answer at end of chapter)

As much as we want our children to be good money managers—to use their allowances wisely, to balance a checkbook and so on—financially intelligent parents provide their children with more than basic money skills. Our kids need to grow up to be *giving* human beings in the best sense of that word. Parents who simply recite the adage "It is better to give than to receive" won't nurture their kids' generous impulses. It takes more than saying the right things to raise a kind, giving child. It's a mistake to view involvement in charity as the province of the wealthy. In reality, many options exist for parents to involve their families in giving activities. Involving kids in charity teaches them that they can do more with money than spend it on themselves. By participating as a family in volunteer and community activities, parents help their kids develop a sense of compassion for and responsibility to others.

Despite all this, some of you may find it more difficult to embrace this money behavior than you might some of our other suggestions. Part of the problem is that becoming a charitable family requires a commitment of time, something that is in short supply in our society. Just as problematic, though, is that it's tough to know where to start. If you've never been involved in volunteer activities and don't have an easy entry point (such as membership in a church group with regularly scheduled volunteer opportunities), finding the right cause or venue can be challenging. Many parents say, "I'd really like to get my family involved in a good cause" but never do anything about it.

Charitable efforts should involve more than giving a dollar to a homeless person. "Living a life of purpose" and "making a difference" are more than just nice-sounding phrases. Happiness actually requires more than making a good living or having good relationships. Jean Chatzky and *Money* magazine engaged RoperASW, a major market research firm, to conduct extensive proprietary research on the influence that money has on an individual's overall happiness. One of the discoveries reported in Chatzky's book, *You Don't Have to Be Rich,* was that people who help others are happier with most aspects of their lives—friendships, marriage, children, lifestyle, financial situation and self-esteem—than those who don't. Finally, kids gain a psychological benefit from giving; it teaches them that they have the power to make life better for others. This empowering lesson will serve them well in many other areas of their lives.

GETTING STARTED: WHEN THEY CAN EMPATHIZE, THEY CAN GIVE

Start introducing your children to the concept of charity at about age four. Until that age, children believe that everyone perceives things the same way they do. A few years ago we were at a shopping mall when we ran into our neighbor Elizabeth and her three-year-old son, Jake, who was terribly excited because Mommy had a new car. Jake dragged us to a window overlooking the parking lot, pointed and said, "See, there it is." The problem was that there were dozens of cars in the parking lot. Because Jake knew which car was Mommy's, he was sure that we would know, too. It isn't until about age four that children start to develop what psychologists call *mindsight*—the ability to "see" another's mind and to realize that other people think differently and possess different feelings. Jake had assumed that we would see the car in the same way that he did.

When children experience the revelation that other people have different feelings and ideas, they begin to develop the capacity for empathy, which is the ability to understand other people's feelings. Empathy forms the basis for compassion and charity.

Psychologists believe that engaging in reflective dialogue with your children—the same reflective dialogue that we talked about in chapter 6—helps build mindsight and empathy by creating what child psychiatrist Dan Siegel calls a "culture of compassion within the family." Laying the foundation for your kids to learn how to reflect on what they are doing also helps them become compassionate and empathic.

Money is a fairly abstract concept for small children; they have difficulty dealing with abstractions and need concrete experiences. Involvement in a volunteer activity, as opposed to writing a check to a charity, is key. Modeling charitable behaviors can jump-start your child's empathy and desire to give. Sherry, for instance, began modeling charitable behavior when her daughter, Tracy, was four. She explained to Tracy that there were many children whose mommies and daddies didn't have the money to buy them toys, and that she might want to gather up the toys she was "too big for" and put them in a bag. Tracy was glad to do this task, and they drove over to a shelter run by a local church; Tracy carried the bag in. As Tracy became older, they would carry out this tradition a few times a year.

Not only did these simple activities show Tracy that her mom was involved in helping the disadvantaged, but they also provided an accessible process through which Tracy could become involved. Giving toys to kids who can't afford them is a concept most young children grasp. Sherry told us that on one or two occasions, Tracy had second thoughts about some toys she had donated and decided to keep a few of them for herself. This is fine. Expect these second thoughts and don't turn a learning experience into a fight. As long as children are willing to give up some of their toys, they are on the right track.

Some older children we interviewed recognized their parents' charitable involvement but found it uninvolving. One teen recalled how his parents made a big deal of giving money to charity when he was younger but said that he and his siblings "didn't feel like we were helping anyone, not like going to a homeless shelter and giving someone a blanket. As a small child you can understand helping others so much more when here is this person who is cold or had dirty clothes and you're giving him a jacket. That way is much easier for a small child to understand. Seeing your parent sign a piece of paper doesn't hit you the same way."

Getting your children involved doesn't require a huge investment of time and effort. Grace and Hal, for instance, took advantage of an existing charitable endeavor in which their older children were involved, an experience that had an especially powerful impact on their four-year-old daughter. Their ten-year-old and twelve-year-old kids attended a local public school that had adopted a homeless shelter. Once a week, both children brought two cans of food to school for the shelter. Grace and Hal decided that the experience would be more meaningful if every family member donated a few hours once a month to work at the shelter. Even their four-year-old daughter helped stack canned goods on the lower shelves. One day, she helped stack canned peaches. That evening, the family served dinner at the shelter, and the meal included canned peaches. Now that a number of years have passed, their younger daughter still recalls how good it made her feel when she was four years old and saw the residents at the homeless shelter eating "her" peaches. Today, all three kids continue to be active volunteers.

HOW TO GET A TEEN TO THINK ABOUT AND DO FOR OTHERS

While younger children will usually follow their parents' lead when it comes to volunteering, teenagers are another story, especially if they weren't involved in these activities when they were younger. In fact, when we conduct our workshops, parents often ask us how to convince a reluctant fourteen- or fifteen-year-old to get involved in good causes. Youth groups are often a good answer.

Andy, age seventeen, grew up in a family where he saw his parents write checks to charity but didn't become personally involved until the ninth grade, when a friend suggested that he join a youth group at the local church. "So I came down and had a fun time. . . . I didn't know that it was going to be more important than just a social experience." When he was in the tenth grade, the church offered a six-day trip sponsored by Amor Ministries in Tijuana, Mexico, to help build houses. "It takes four days to build a house," said Andy. "The first day is leveling out and pouring the foundation. We mix all the cement by hand because it is kind of culturally ineffective to come in with an electric mixer. It's not like we're doing the work; it's like our fancy machines are doing the work; so, instead, we mix in bins with hoes. The second day is building the frame of the house; basically it's wood and nails all day. The next day you put baling wire around the whole house and then tar paper, and then the fourth and final day we stucco the house, mix some more cement, and we also finish the roof."

We asked Andy whether, when he had kids of his own, he wanted them to become volunteers. Here's Andy's answer, word for word:

> *Definitely, so that they know that a real joy can be found, not through money and not through getting something new, but just spending time doing something worthwhile, helping other people. It doesn't have to be something that is not fun or burdensome. A lot of times when people ask me, "What did you do over spring break?" I'll say, "I went to Mexico"; they'll say, "Oh, Cancun; did you relax on the beaches?" I'll say, "Well, not exactly; we were working building houses." And they will say, "Oh, how nice of you to give up your spring break." But I don't feel that I'm giving up my spring break. I feel that I am doing something that would make me happier than just relaxing because it makes me feel good, significant. It's not just about me. I like that. Knowing that we are doing something worthwhile and significant brings a sense of contentment that is really hard to find anywhere else.*

Andy also felt that he would want his kids to get involved earlier than the ninth grade, but he offered this observation:

> *I would start my kids earlier but I would probably want to accompany them if they were younger, just so that if they had questions, I'd be there. Because I could see how coming into poverty can be really upsetting, and I wouldn't want to fill a child with despair, because it's better to focus on what we can do as opposed to what we can't do. So, if my child asked why it is like this, I would help him or her understand that we can't fix all the problems, but we can start little by little. It would be important for me to be there with my child.*

Most teenagers are open to charitable opportunities, especially when they are working in concert with other teens. If you tell your sixteen-year-old out of the blue that you want her to drive down to a local soup kitchen and work there every Saturday, she'll probably resist your suggestion. You're asking her to do too much too fast. A much better approach is to take the following steps:

1. *Do a little research on your own to determine what youth-oriented volunteering opportunities exist in your area. Churches and other religious institutions almost always have some ongoing programs. Schools often have eco-clubs and other charitable activities.*

2. *Discuss your research with your child and help her create a list of opportunities for involvement that appeal to her: some kids like the adventure of going overseas to build houses; others are more interested in doing something closer to home or in an area where they have a particular skill—your daughter might be a softball player who teaches the game to kids with developmental disabilities, for instance. Look for opportunities to involve the entire family.*

3. *Once your teenager is involved, ask her about the experience periodically. Give her the chance to explore her feelings about helping others, her fears or concerns related to poverty, death or disease and her pride in taking part in selfless acts.*

WHY YOUR GIVING BEHAVIOR IS MORE IMPORTANT THAN YOU MIGHT THINK

In the vast majority of cases, compassionate, giving adults raise compassionate, giving children. But if your child rarely witnesses behaviors that reflect your belief in the importance of charity, your caring will have less impact. Therefore, don't overlook the importance of seizing opportunities to show your child your giving side. When you see a can on a restaurant counter seeking donations to cure a disease, drop some money in the slot. When you receive mail soliciting funds for a cause you believe in, tell your child about it and ask how much he thinks you should give. When there's a walk or race designed to benefit a good cause, participate as a family. The net effect will help your child live a purposeful existence, not only throughout his childhood but also when he is an adult.

Our friends Art and Penny modeled charitable behavior in many ways. Their story is especially unusual in that their son, Scott, died at age seventeen because of a congenital heart condition. Given Scott's four major heart operations and the knowledge that his life might be short, he could have understandably become focused on his own problems. It is to his parents' credit—not to mention Scott's own considerable courage—that this was not the case. He lived a full life in a short period of time, and helping others was a major part of that life. Scott saw that volunteering was important to his parents. When Scott was three, his parents donated some of their time to help at his preschool. Scott would get tired of playing in the sandbox and would come over to help Mommy and Daddy paint a wall. He wasn't a particularly good painter, but he tried, and when he became bored painting, he'd go back to playing with his friends. When he was six or so, Scott and his mother were listening to the car radio when they heard about a police officer who was shot. He was a single father and had a young son. Scott felt so bad that he wanted to donate some of the money he had saved from his allowance. Art and Penny told Scott that they would match whatever he donated. Scott attended the local public school and, as at most school districts in the 1990s, funds were tight and schools began to cut back on activities. Penny worked as a paralegal Monday through Thursday. On Fridays, she volunteered at the school and sometimes helped supervise the computer lab. Scott saw that on days no parents volunteered, there was no computer lab. When he got to Venice High School in Los Angeles, he helped two friends start Komputers4Kids, which collected and refurbished old computers and donated them to group and foster homes for children. A few weeks before he passed away, Scott was named outstanding youth volunteer for the 2003 National Philanthropy Day Award of the Heart Association. When we asked Art and Penny why Scott was so involved in helping others when he was suffering from a life-threatening condition, they said simply, "We always did things as a family, and children pick up on what they see."

All of us know that role models play an important part in our children's lives. It was only ten years ago, though, that scientists found out why, as a result of an Italian researcher who wanted an ice cream cone and a chimpanzee who ended up eating it!

Marco Iacoboni is an associate professor at the UCLA Neuropsychiatric Institute. Ten years ago, he was in Italy, engaged in a research project that involved hooking up a chimp to an electroencephalograph (EEG), a device that records the electrical impulses in the brain. It was a hot day and Iacoboni took a break to buy one of those wonderful Italian gelato cones. When he came back to the lab and started to lick the gelato cone, the EEG showed a bunch of neurons firing in the chimp's brain. Iacoboni stopped licking the cone, and the neurons stopped firing in the chimp's brain. He took another lick, and the same neurons fired. He stopped; the neurons stopped firing in the chimp's brain. Iacoboni handed the cone to the chimp. The chimp started licking it and the same neurons fired!

Research on humans showed exactly the same result. Iacoboni had discovered mirror neurons. Chimps have them. So do we.

Our brains are built out of about a hundred billion or so long, narrow cells called neurons. Neurons have thousands of connections at each end and "talk" to one another through tiny electrical impulses that jump from connection to connection. When a neuron sends an electrical impulse to another neuron, it is said to be *firing*. Thinking and memory actually consist of neurons talking to one another through these electrical impulses.

What Iacoboni discovered was that if we engage in an intentional activity, such as licking an ice cream cone or giving money to a homeless person, an observer will have the same brain activity that would have occurred had she been licking the cone or giving the money! When Iacoboni decided to lick the cone, neurons in his brain started firing. Some of them told his arm to contract and bring the cone to his mouth. Others told his tongue to lick the cone. Because the chimp was watching him, the same neurons in the chimp's brain started firing even though the chimp didn't move his arm and stick out his tongue.

The existence of mirror neurons makes all types of parental modeling behaviors important, especially when it comes to charitable behavior. In this day and age, children are extremely vulnerable to a hedonistic, self-absorbed lifestyle. The cynicism and irony that dominates much of the music they listen to and the television shows they watch can steer them away from good causes. The media doesn't show people who are cool and hip spending their time working in soup kitchens or trying to help others less fortunate. Instead, they focus on satisfying their need to dress in the latest styles or to provide themselves with temporary escapes through drugs and alcohol.

When you model charitable giving, though, you provide your kids with a defense against these societal messages. You give them an alternative to the jaded, self-indulgent pose of some of their peers.

EXPLAIN WHY AND MAKE IT REAL

As important as it is to model giving behaviors, it's just as important to provide kids with a context for a given charitable act and help them see its real-world impact. Context means giving your kids a reason to get involved. This doesn't mean just explaining why, but choosing a particular activity where the reason naturally emerges. For instance, if your child's grandparent has a particular disease, participating in a walk to fund research on that disease provides children with an obvious reason. Scott had built-in context: he was born with a heart condition, and one of the major recipients of his volunteer efforts was Camp Del Corazon, a summer camp for children with heart disease located on Catalina Island, twenty-two miles off the coast of Southern California. When you and your child watch a television program about a local shelter for battered women and children, you can engage your child in a discussion about how fortunate you are to live in a safe environment and how you can help the shelter by volunteering or fundraising. You can also involve your child in helping an elderly neighbor obtain food at the store or clean up his yard; your child will quickly grasp that the elderly neighbor needs assistance because of his age or infirmities.

Seth, age eighteen, has parents who were adept at communicating the reason behind their family's charitable efforts. From the time he was little, his parents made sure Seth comprehended why they were helping others and what specific needs they were meeting. All this came to fruition when Seth was in high school and one of his classmates was diagnosed with multiple sclerosis. He explained:

> *My friend was suffering and I wanted to help. It was the first time I really understood the importance of helping others and it became part of my daily life. It wasn't just trying to raise money to help find a cure. Some days she would have more trouble walking than others and would have to take the elevator to get to the second floor. I didn't want her to ride the elevator alone so I'd go with her. Unless you really get involved, you really aren't helping.*

Making it real is the second goal, and it simply means turning a donation or indirect charitable action into something that kids can experience directly. For instance, if your child contributes money to the local zoo to help provide a new habitat for the kangaroo, be involved yourself and, when it's completed, take your child to see the kangaroo's new home. If you have your child lick stamps and seal envelopes for a mailing designed to alert the community to the existence of an environment polluter in your midst, you should also take a family trip to see the dark smoke coming out of a smokestack or a river that smells and looks toxic. Abstract concepts are not effective with younger children. Though you may be able to paint a good verbal picture, there is no substitute for seeing something with your own two eyes, no matter what age you are.

HOW TO BECOME A CHARITABLE FAMILY

Giving your kids a context for giving and making the experience real are behaviors that will help you become a charitable family. Charitable families are highly conscious of opportunities to give, and they make the most of them. Volunteering strengthens family relationships and teaches kids such values as kindness, empathy and respect for others, and, perhaps even more important, it teaches that happiness is not dependent on what we have. During a break in a workshop we were conducting in Atlanta, a mother told us about a recent trip to Mexico where her entire family spent a week helping at an orphanage. Her ten-year-old son, John, subsequently wrote an essay that captures the value of volunteering far better than anything we could say:

It is important to know how fortunate we are. I learned this life lesson last year over spring break when we worked at a Mexican orphanage. The house where we stayed had no air-conditioning and no hot water. At the orphanage I saw that their soccer "field" was made of bricks and had torn-up goals. Two children had to sleep together in each twin bed. They didn't get any snacks and they had to eat all their dinner before playing. Some of the children only had one pair of shoes which were nice school shoes. They took them off while playing soccer because they didn't want to ruin their shoes. The orphanage didn't have an iron and when a boy at the orphanage got his first job he bought the orphanage an iron. The thing I thought was amazing, and what changed me, was that these children were happy even with practically no toys or other possessions. They are happy because they live in a safe environment now with people that take good care of them. My trip to Mexico showed I am really blessed.

A hallmark of charitable families is volunteerism. As a parent, you need to make a consistent effort to involve your entire family in activities that benefit others. This doesn't mean you have to devote every spare moment to good works or that you have to be dictatorial and declare to your family, "Get off your butts and start helping others!" The responsibility of a financially intelligent parent, though, is to provide options for and initiate interest in activities. Here are some possibilities to help you get started:

- *Visit seniors in hospitals or nursing homes.*
- *Help clean up at the local park.*
- *Become a volunteer tutor in a literacy project—especially great if your child is bilingual.*
- *Join a local conservation organization and participate in its activities.*
- *Get involved in playtime and reading stories at a children's shelter.*
- *Become a storyteller in a children's reading program at the local library.*
- *Teach basic computer skills at a senior center.*
- *Help maintain a local bike path or hiking trail.*

If you are looking for volunteer opportunities for your family, there are many resources available to you, especially if you have an Internet connection. VolunteerMatch (www.volunteermatch.org) provides a database of volunteer activities that can be searched by zip code and sorted by activities that are great for kids, teens, seniors or groups. When we input our zip code in Los Angeles and asked for volunteer opportunities within twenty miles of our house, VolunteerMatch came up with 64 hits for kids, 314 volunteer possibilities for teens and 346 hits for groups! Action Without Borders, located in New York, maintains the Idealist.org Web site (www.idealist.org), which offers the ability to match volunteers with as many as thirty-six thousand nonprofits worldwide. The International Association for Volunteer Effort is an international nongovernmental organization that promotes volunteerism worldwide. Its Web site (www.iave.org) contains links to volunteer organizations in more than eighty countries.

Family involvement in charity doesn't require money, and it can lead to great things. A great example comes from Deborah Spaide, whose decision to have her family paint an elderly woman's apartment led to the creation of more than eight hundred Kids Care Clubs throughout the United States. Deborah grew up in a working-class community in Maine, where she worked afternoons at her father's hardware store. Some of the families were so poor that they couldn't afford to buy washers to repair kitchen faucets. The community was tight-knit, and she had the firsthand experience of seeing families helping one another. In 1989 Deborah and her husband, Jim, a successful business consultant, moved with their five children to an affluent community in Connecticut. They quickly became concerned about the values that their children were being exposed to, and even more concerned that their kids had no contact with poor people. They decided that the entire family would get involved in helping others as a team. They began by painting the apartment of an elderly woman in a neighboring community; the apartment had not been painted during the entire twenty years she lived there. A few weeks later the kids decided to help out another elderly lady who couldn't afford anyone to help with yard work. Deborah and Jim said that each of the kids could invite one friend to help. Fifteen kids showed up at their door, armed with rakes. Then the same kids made 150 bag lunches for a nearby soup kitchen. Pretty soon they had fifty boys and girls meeting each week in their kitchen discussing the next projects that they would be doing. When Deborah and Jim asked them what they wanted to be called, they came up with the name Kids Care Club. The nearby middle school started letting the kids meet there. Soon all the public schools in the nearby area had Kids Care Clubs.

In 2003, the projects of the eight hundred Kids Care Clubs reached an estimated 3.6 million people and distributed more than $1.7 million in relief. To find the Kids Care Club nearest you—or to get help in starting your own—visit the club Web site: www.kidscare.org.

Too often, kids grow up feeling disempowered, convinced that they can't have much of an impact on a world outside of school until they are adults. As a financially intelligent parent, you can teach them otherwise.

Not only children can be entrepreneurial volunteers. You should practice what we call *creative volunteerism*. In other words, don't limit yourself to traditional charitable activities. Use your imagination to transform events and situations into opportunities for giving. Not only can this make charitable efforts fun, but it also communicates to your children that being creative can result in more meaningful giving.

One example of creative charity involves friends of ours in Los Angeles who throw an annual holiday party. Their house is beautifully decorated. The invitation tells you to bring an unwrapped present suitable for a mother or a child under age ten. When you drive up, you hand the present to a man dressed as Santa Claus, who places it in one of several large cardboard boxes. The next day, our friends and their teenage daughter personally deliver the presents to a local shelter for battered women and children.

Similarly, birthdays, holidays and special events can provide a charitable option for attendees. The Center for a New American Dream (www.newdream.org) offers "Tips for Parenting in a Commercial Culture" and "Simplify the Holidays." One tip offered is to opt out of giving "things" as birthday gifts; if your child agrees, give him a gift certificate redeemable as a donation in his name to a charity. You might also sound him out about asking guests to bring toys that can be donated to a children's shelter. An older child might be interested in earmarking a certain percentage of the money received for a graduation, bar mitzvah or other celebration as a donation to a charitable group.

You can also be creative with your child's allowance. Though we'll talk in greater detail about allowances in chapter 8, the relevant point here is that you can talk with your child about using part of her allowance for charity. For instance, let's say you give your kid five dollars per week. Add an extra fifty cents to the allowance and explain to your child that this money is for her to give to a charity she wants to support. Fifty cents each week adds up to twenty-six dollars she can give to charity each year. To a seven-year-old, twenty-six dollars is a lot of money. Take your child to visit the organization to see how her money was spent. Maybe it went to help build that new home for the kangaroo at the zoo. That's a powerful lesson for your child: Her contribution is important. Here's another suggestion: Before sending in the money, make sure there is someone at the organization who will write a thank-you note to your child. When the note arrives, make sure your child opens it and reads it to the entire family. Not only does this reinforce your child's involvement, but it creates another teachable moment: Ask how the thank-you note makes her feel and then use that to explain why it is important for her to write thank-you notes when other people do nice things for her—give her a birthday gift, for example.

OVERCOMING INERTIA, MAINTAINING MOMENTUM

If you're like most parents, you want to model these giving behaviors but you lack the time or energy to turn your wishes into action. It may also be that you've tried to get your family involved in a volunteer effort, but after an initial burst of participation, the family's interest flagged. To overcome the inertia or maintain the momentum of this money behavior, we've created two approaches that you might want to try.

Overcoming Inertia—The Excuse Eliminator

The following is a list of the top seven excuses people give to explain why they aren't more involved in charitable activities. Note which ones apply to you.

1. I am too exhausted from work to get myself or my family to volunteer for anything.
2. The only time I have to volunteer is weekends, and weekends are for relaxing and fun activities.
3. My spouse and kids will never go along with my volunteering suggestions.
4. I can't find a cause or activity that will suit everyone in my family.
5. We regularly give money to a number of good causes; that's enough.
6. We just don't have the time; our schedules are filled.
7. I want to wait until my kids are teenagers and are better able to understand why it's important to help others in need.

The following are responses to each excuse, designed to get you into action and involved in a good cause (numbered excuses correspond to numbered responses):

1. *Most people find volunteer work to be energizing. Because it is so different from what both adults and children usually are doing and because it has a clear, positive goal, people become revved up and engaged. It is nothing like a job or schoolwork, and people leave volunteering activities more energized than when they started.*

2. *Charitable participation is often fun. Weekends are frequently the time that walks, bike rides and races for good causes are held. In addition, kids can find it enjoyable to work in a soup kitchen or help clean up the environment. These aren't sedentary, clock-watching tasks, but ones in which kids are in new environments meeting people they don't normally meet.*

3. *Your spouse and kids won't go along with your suggestions if you dictate them. Instead of telling them which volunteer*

effort you want them to participate in, ask for their ideas. Or you might use the ideas in this chapter to give them a host of options for participation.

4. *The previous response is one way to deal with this excuse. Another way is to try different activities until you find one that everyone enjoys. You can plan a rotation in which you spend the first quarter of the year volunteering at one place, then switch to a new group each quarter.*

5. *As we've emphasized, writing checks is great, but it's insufficient if you want to be a financially intelligent parent. Ask yourself if you want your kids to view you as saying the right things (about giving) but not practicing what you preach. Remember, when it comes to being a financially intelligent parent,* later is now!

6. *This is probably the most common excuse, and the best way to eliminate it is to designate one hour per week as "giving time." Everyone can spare one hour. Have everyone in your family make a commitment of one hour to volunteer or serve others in some way.*

7. *Remind yourself that if you wait until your kids are teenagers, it's going to be much more difficult to get them involved in charitable activities than if you start them off when they are young.*

Maintaining Momentum—The Rewards and Recognitions Program

Understandably, volunteer activities sometimes take a backseat to more pressing concerns: a child's involvement in sports, schoolwork and hobbies such as music or art. You may also have events in your life that take you away from giving activities, such as a new, time-consuming job or more travel. Nonetheless, maintaining a consistent level of involvement may be easier if you put the following rewards and recognitions program into effect:

- *When you do volunteer activities with your kids, discuss these activities and tell them how and why they're making valuable contributions. Don't assume that they'll understand that they're doing good. Pointing out that you're proud of them and the specific ways in which they've helped a given individual or group will validate their participation and increase the odds that they'll stick with it.*

- *Start small and build involvement rather than making a huge commitment of your family's time. If you try to do too much too fast, you'll probably alienate your kids. They're going to feel resentful if you suddenly insist that they devote each Saturday to working on an environmental cleanup project while their friends are doing whatever they want. Ideally, you'll start with a small commitment of time and it will build naturally. Maybe you start them off with one small project that naturally leads to other projects. Once people get involved in a cause, opportunities for additional involvement usually arise. Your children will become aware of the issues involved as well as the different activities and groups that are trying to make things better; they may well identify a particular program or project that suits them and to which they want to devote additional time. The reward here is that they feel like they want to be more involved rather than that involvement is being forced upon them.*

- *Watch for signs that your kids are getting bored and try to make the activity a more positive experience. Is the initial enthusiasm your children exhibited when you began volunteering starting to fade? Are they asking, "Do we have to?" before you leave for a volunteer activity? Do they seem to be suffering in silence as you drive toward the shelter? If so, it may be time to switch volunteer activities. Find something more to their liking. Perhaps they would prefer joining an environmental group rather than working at a shelter because global warming is what has them concerned. Perhaps you can find a time for these activities that better suits their schedules.*

- *Add a fun element to volunteering. Realistically, some charitable activities may involve tedious or repetitive work. No one said that doing good for others is all fun and games. At the same time, you can help your children look forward to these activities by adding something that makes it more fun. For instance, you might schedule a family breakfast at a favorite pancake house before working in a shelter on Saturday morning. You might look for a museum, hiking trail or other family activity near where the volunteering is taking place, combining the two activities. At the same time, don't turn these rewards into bribes; don't say, "If you volunteer, I'll take you to the amusement park." Instead, take advantage of the proximity of fun places or create an enjoyable ritual out of volunteering.*

Ultimately, the best reward for volunteering is internal. Sooner or later, your children will feel as if they're spending their time on something meaningful, that they are doing something that really matters to others. Sometimes it takes a while for this realization to dawn on them. When it does, though, you've achieved a significant breakthrough. You have helped your children learn that everything in life doesn't revolve around them and satisfying their own needs. You have given them the chance to feel good by focusing on other people. This is a great life lesson, and one that financially intelligent parents are able to teach effectively.

Answer to Financially Intelligent Brainteaser

This is the only brainteaser that has two right answers. Though answer A might provide a life-changing experience for your kids, it could also be too much to start with. Answer B is fine, but it involves simply giving money rather than active participation. Answers C and D are both good. Both offer the

opportunity for the entire family to participate together. Answer C also includes other children your kids know, and it's a project that they can relate to and that will require continuing involvement over time. Answer D provides context for involvement. Although it is a one-time event, you will get on the organization's mailing list, which will provide you and your children with other opportunities for involvement. ◆

8

TEACH FINANCIAL LITERACY

Financially Intelligent Brainteaser

Your child has just turned eleven, and you feel he is ready to take on more responsibilities around the house. Though he already helps out in some ways—he mows the lawn and shovels snow in the winter—you have certain additional projects in mind for him. You have an older home that is in need of repairs, and it strikes you that he could be of great assistance—scraping paint from the woodwork, helping repair a broken sprinkler and so on. You're not sure how to compensate him for this additional work, but you're considering the following options:

A. Telling him that he is going to receive a 25 percent increase in his allowance for doing these special projects
B. Keeping him at the same allowance but telling him he doesn't have to mow the lawn or shovel the snow anymore
C. Telling him to do the additional chores without any additional compensation
D. Forging a separate agreement in which you pay him a specific amount for each additional chore while maintaining his allowance

(Answer at end of chapter)

Raising financially intelligent kids is a two-dimensional process rather than a one-time lecture. Put another way, you can't teach your child to be financially intelligent simply by helping him learn to balance a checkbook or create a budget. While these skills are important and we'll focus on how to teach them effectively, they must be taught within the context of values and money relationships. If, for instance, you teach your child how to use a credit card and then give her a card with no limits that allows her to buy anything she wants whenever she wants it, you're helping her acquire a skill without giving her the values to use it appropriately.

Don't plan a condensed series of talks about budgeting, bank accounts, investing and the like. While it's great to help your children acquire knowledge about all these subjects, it's just knowledge. Forcing children to study the stock market or know the ins and outs of real estate investments may help them become savvy investors—though this point is debatable—but it won't teach them one thing about financial responsibility. Our point is that you should couple the information you convey to your kids about financial management with opportunities for learning about responsibility and decision making.

MANAGING MONEY AND MANAGING LIFE

Approach financial management lessons as an opportunity to teach your children both money skills and life skills. When they learn to deal with an allowance by creating budgets and engaging in reflective thinking before spending money, they become better able to make choices and assume responsibility for their actions. Matt, for instance, is a fourteen-year-old who has learned to think in terms of consequences and relationships. His first recollection of money is his parents giving him a quarter when he was four or so, and his realization that he could trade that quarter for his favorite food group: a gum ball. By the time he was in third grade, he had saved two hundred dollars from his allowance. Why? Because when he thinks about spending money, he asks himself, "Do I want this or do I really need this?" Listen to Matt talk at age fourteen, and you'll discover that he has learned a lesson from managing his allowance money that translates into other areas of life:

If you are going to buy a movie, are you going to watch it more than once? Because if you are not, then just rent it. Whereas all the movies that I have bought I watch all the time. I can rent the ones that aren't funny because I am probably not going to watch it again if it's not funny. But if it is a funny movie it will be funny more than once. I have movies that I have seen probably at least twenty times. The only videos I buy are comedies. I know I'll watch them more than once and my friends will watch them with me. I don't buy dramas; I only want to watch them once, so why waste the money? I don't only think this way about money. I think this way about food. I try to eat healthy so I don't trash my body. Every once in a while I can have dessert if I have a good dinner.

Matt's ideas about money and consequences may not seem like a big deal within the context of a young adolescent's life, but they provide the foundation for making other good life decisions. Similarly, parents who encourage their children to invest some of their allowance—rather than just telling them about investing—help them learn how to manage risk. When investing, people must decide between financial markets, where the potential for both gain and loss is relatively high, or a safer investment, where there is less risk but also less opportunity for gain. After financially intelligent parents educate their children about investments and show them the options available, kids will do the rest. Thoughts similar to this one will run through their heads:

Should I invest my money so it's safe or so it grows? Maybe I should do both and put some of the money in a safe investment and some in a riskier investment offering a higher reward.

Even if your child makes a mistake, he'll learn from it. Not only will he discover that he can lose all his money if he makes a bad, risky investment—not a bad lesson to learn if you're only investing twenty dollars—but he'll also start thinking about other choices in his life and their accompanying risk-reward scenarios. The very notion of taking responsibility for making a bad choice—of telling yourself that you messed up this time but you won't mess up in the same way again—is a sign of resilience and maturity.

Given the lessons to be learned from teaching your children basic money-management skills, where do you start? The first and best place is allowances.

THREE GREAT WAYS TO MAKE ALLOWANCES WORK FOR YOUR KIDS

It's easy to make mistakes when it comes to allowances. Some parents don't believe in them and just give their kids money whenever they ask for something. Other parents don't believe in them because they assume their kids will squander the money. Still others believe in allowances but give their children too much or too little. It's so easy to be financially *un*intelligent when it comes to allowances. To avoid making a mistake, review these three recommendations:

Recommendation 1: All Children Should Receive an Allowance

It is not that you'll psychologically scar your child if you don't give her an allowance. You will, however, fail to capitalize on a powerful tool to help your child learn to think reflectively. Consider what happens when you give your child an allowance. Every week when you hand her money, she has a taste of freedom and independence. She is responsible for spending the money as she chooses. She is the one who decides not only what to spend it on, but what to save for. Psychologically, allowances give kids the opportunity to make choices in more mature ways than their age might normally allow.

Recall the marshmallow test. Remember how kids who were able to think reflectively and delay gratification were more socially competent, less likely to go to pieces under stress, better able to deal with challenges and more self-reliant and, on average, scored 210 points higher on their SAT tests than those who were unable to delay gratification? Allowances help kids learn to think reflectively. Faced with a fixed amount of money to spend, even a six-year-old learns to mull over her choices and consider the consequences in a rudimentary way. If she doesn't, she will run out of money before she runs out of week. Don't rush in and rescue her by buying what she wants but can't afford because she already spent her allowance. Allow her to absorb the wisdom of thinking before spending.

At what age should an allowance begin? When kids become interested in money and understand the concept that you exchange money for goods or services—usually around age five or six—it's time. Children who see older brothers or sisters receiving an allowance tend to get interested in money and want an allowance earlier than an only child. If they have a set amount to spend, they have to ask themselves: "Should I spend my money on gum balls or save it to buy a video game?" That may not sound like the world's most important question, but it's the start of learning self-discipline. Allowances permit us to talk with—and not just to—our children about money and values. You can lecture your kids all you want about spending money on meaningful purchases, but it's not until your child has an allowance and blows all his money on a toy he quickly grows tired of (and perhaps breaks) that values come into play. "I want to buy that model airplane, Daddy. I love building those planes," your child says. "That's what I really want, not that dumb thing that broke." Valuing purchases that reflect who you really are and what counts in your life—these lessons all flow naturally when you give your child an allowance.

Be aware, too, that allowances present financially intelligent parents with a chance to identify their own unresolved money issues—issues that may hamper their ability to teach their kids how to manage money and convey the right values. If, for instance, you are an overspender, you may give your child so much allowance money that it fosters a sense of entitlement. If you have serious money-management issues, you could force your child to account for every penny of allowance spent, giving rise to anxiety that can trouble your child into adulthood. Therefore, pay attention to your behavior around allowances. Talk with and observe your spouse regarding these behaviors. If they seem extreme—if most people you know give their ten-year-old children five to ten dollars per week and you're giving your kid fifty—then adjust your behavior so that it falls more within the normal range.

Recommendation 2: Allowances Should Not Be Tied to Chores

Chores are done because kids are members of the family and everyone helps out. Viewed this way, chores help kids develop a work ethic. On the other hand, allowances help them learn to manage money and think reflectively. While both are positive goals, they shouldn't be mixed. If your child learns to view his allowance as payment for doing his chores, you are sending conflicting signals—he is expected to help out because he is a member of the family, but he gets paid for helping out. You are also using external motivation, a system of rewards and punishments, to control your child's behavior rather than allowing him to develop an inner drive to do well. (You are preventing him from becoming autotelic.)

Every parent knows that kids don't always do their chores. When they don't, there have to be consequences. The consequences, however, should not be tied to money. When you link consequences to the allowance, you are doing the last thing that a financially intelligent parent should be doing: Teaching kids that money is a reward for "good" behavior and a punishment for "bad" behavior.

To understand how this allowance recommendation fosters financial responsibility, view it through the lens of the five childhood developmental stages. These stages are like a five-story building: each story builds on a foundation created by the lower floors. The first floor is trust. Around age two or so, your child starts building the second floor, which is autonomy: the belief that she is capable of becoming a separate and autonomous person. The process of building this floor isn't completed by age four. It continues throughout her lifetime. If she doesn't succeed in building this second floor securely, the remaining three floors will be swaying in the breeze. Autonomy is furthered when your child develops a sense of internal satisfaction from doing a good job. Substituting money for a sense of satisfaction interferes with your child's ability to create an internal system that allows her to make good decisions.

Approaching allowances the right way allows us to instill decision-making wisdom in our children as opposed to controlling them. Stuart Ende, a psychoanalyst in Los Angeles, has observed that parents can use external threats and bribery to make their kids act morally, but it won't have the effect of making them moral. Rewards and punishments are an external structure. You aren't helping your children figure out for themselves what is and what isn't moral behavior. Once your kids move out and the rewards and punishments aren't there anymore, they no longer have a system in place to distinguish between right and wrong.

We would bet that the young adults who get themselves in credit card debt are overwhelmingly children of parents who used allowances for rewards and punishments. Though we know of no study to this effect, it makes perfect psychological sense that this would be the case. It's likely that these children came from homes where parents used money to control their behaviors; they provided an external structure that guided their kids' actions when it came to spending. When the kids left home, they also left this structure behind and had no internal structure to guide them. As a result, they max out their credit cards, find themselves in dire financial straits and end up moving back home with their parents, perhaps in an unconscious effort to restore the external structure imposed in adolescence.

As parents, we all become frustrated with our children's behaviors at times, and our reflex is to try to get them to do the right thing by offering or taking away something they value. The problem, of course, is that if you use money for this purpose, your kids begin to view money as a punishment or a reward. They grow up believing that they should work primarily for money; they begin to measure their self-worth by how much they are paid.

To avoid sending this message, consider the following dialogue Eileen had with the mother of a misbehaving eight-year-old at one of our workshops:

MOTHER: "If I can't take my eight-year-old son's allowance away, how can I punish him when he does something wrong?"

EILEEN: *"What's he doing wrong?"*

MOTHER: "He keeps going outside without his shoes on and getting his white socks dirty. I've been fining him three dollars each time he does it."

EILEEN: *"Does it work?"*

MOTHER: "No, he keeps doing it."

EILEEN: *"Look at his behavior. He's not misusing money; he's misusing his socks. So why are you using money as a punishment? The next time he gets his white socks dirty, give him a box of detergent and tell him to keep washing them by hand until they are clean."*

We received an e-mail from the mother a few months later. She had to follow Eileen's advice only once. That was the last time her son went outside without his shoes on.

Recommendation 3: If You Want to Figure Out How Much the Allowance Should Be, Think About the Length of Abe Lincoln's Legs

Fostering financial responsibility through allowances depends on giving your child the right amount of allowance. If you give her too much, it fosters a financially irresponsible mind-set because there's no need for her to make wise decisions about how to spend money. If you give her too little, it also encourages irresponsibility because there's not enough money available for her to make wise choices possible. Just as significantly, many parents view allowances as token payments to kids for things such as candy and movies. They fail to see the opportunity to make the allowance a more meaningful tool.

When it comes to figuring out how much allowance to give your kids, we suggest taking Abe Lincoln's advice to heart. At six foot four,

Abe was very tall by the standards of the mid-1800s, and most of his height was in his very long legs. One day a newspaper reporter asked him how long people's legs should be. Abe contemplated the question and then replied that since legs were designed to allow people to walk, they should be long enough to reach from their body to the ground! In the same way, allowances should be enough to help your child learn to manage money responsibly.

Clever, eh? But how do you figure this out?

First, calculate what you are spending on your child, with an eye toward turning over some responsibility for the spending through his allowance. Get a notebook small enough to carry around in a purse or a pocket and jot down what you buy for your kids during the week and how much it costs: candy, trading cards, CDs, toys and anything else you spend on them. If you are married, have your spouse do the same calculation. If you are a single parent and your child lives part of the week with you and part of the week with your ex, ask your ex to keep track, too. Once you've accumulated at least two weeks' worth of information, divide the list into two categories: items you'll continue to pay for, and items the allowance will cover and which will become your child's responsibility. Come up with a fair amount, one that will cover his expenses and give him enough financial leeway to make spending decisions.

Give your child a weekly allowance, rather than a daily or monthly distribution of funds. It's a hassle to hand out money every day, and smaller kids will have difficulty keeping track of money over a period longer than a week. Let's say that you have reviewed the list of expenditures and see that you usually spend a dollar a week on candy for your six-year-old son and another two to three dollars a week on baseball cards. So you decide to start him with a four-dollar-a-week allowance. Giving your child the experience of spending his own money is empowering. It is also a wonderful reality check that teaches him if he spends money today, he'll have less to spend tomorrow. When we asked Tim, age fourteen, what lessons he had learned from having an allowance, he replied, "Each time I spend a dollar, I have the feeling of the money leaving my hand. My wallet is thinner!"

Don't agonize over finding the ideal allowance amount; it's not going to make much of a difference if you give your child a little too much or a bit less than the perfect amount. As long as you come close to the midpoint, it will give your child enough money to meet specific spending requirements and a little left over to make additional buying or saving decisions (you can also offer him the opportunity to do extra chores to make additional money, as suggested in chapter 4).

In addition to following these three recommendations, communicate the rationale for a given allowance. The more your kids feel the allowance is fair, the more likely they'll think before they spend. Therefore, sit down with your children and explain that the allowance is designed to help them pay for items that you used to pay for. Be very specific, especially with little kids: "This means that Mom and I aren't going to be buying your gum balls and trading cards anymore." Make it clear, though, that with this financial responsibility comes financial freedom. As long as the purchase isn't illegal, immoral or harmful to themselves or others, kids should decide what they want to buy. Of course, if your child is obese and wants to spend all of his allowance on junk food, you have the right to say no. But if you force your kids to seek your permission before making every purchase, you aren't teaching them anything except that you are a control freak. They have no incentive to think long term. Being solely responsible for how they spend their allowance—and whether they spend it or save it—helps children develop a sense of autonomy. If you want to keep control over an area of purchases, such as school clothing or computer games, don't include it in the categories covered by the allowance.

With younger children, some families like to spell out that with a five-dollar allowance, for example, one dollar goes to savings, one dollar goes to charity and three dollars is for spending as they see fit. A verbal explanation, however, probably isn't enough. You need to make this division of funds tangible. Therefore, give them the allowance in the form of five one-dollar bills and let them physically divide the allowance into at least three categories: saving, charity and spending. While there are various devices you can use to hold these three different types of monies, we like the Money Savvy Pig, available from www.moneysavvygeneration.com. It comes in various colors and is translucent, so kids can see the money inside it. It even has a fourth money chamber, for investing.

Be aware, too, that allowances should not be set in stone. As kids become older, you need to increase the allowance amounts and decrease the frequency. When you give your child a raise, however, be sure to talk about why she's receiving it and the additional expenditures it's designed to cover. Shifting increasing purchasing responsibility to your child is key, demonstrating your trust in her judgment. When you observe your child gaining some maturity about money matters, extend the allowance frequency to twice a month—similar to how often many employees receive paychecks—and to once a month by the time your son or daughter is in high school. Learning the discipline of making a modest sum of money last a month can be a challenge, but it's one that will pay off in smart money behaviors when your child leaves home.

Finally, consider giving your child—especially a child in middle school or high school—a separate clothing allowance. It's easy to get into battles with kids over clothes, and a separate allowance can help minimize these fights. Clothes have tremendous symbolic importance for teenagers, and while they may be fiscally responsible in other areas of their lives, they can easily blow their entire month's allowance on clothing. A separate clothing allowance prevents this from happening, and it also gives them control of something that has great meaning in their lives.

Provide your kids with a clothing allowance that covers the clothes they need for one semester at school. Specify which types of clothing are covered by the allowance: school clothes, after-school clothes, party clothes, formal clothes, and so on. Try to let your child have as much autonomy in buying clothes as possible. If his school requires uniforms, buy school clothes for him and provide a clothing allowance for after-school clothes. If you want your fourteen-year-old son to have a nice suit to wear on formal family occasions, pay for it yourself and let him use the clothing allowance to buy what he is interested in wearing.

As with the regular allowance, it's important to find a good midpoint figure, one that doesn't allow your child to buy everything she wants but gives her enough leeway to buy a reasonable number of shoes, outfits and so on. To find the right clothing allowance figure, price some outfits at a place where your child likes to shop or in a brand she likes wearing. Determine what your child needs and wants to buy in a given year based on what she has bought in the past, and come up with a realistic budget.

Elyse has observed her daughter, Katrina, use a clothing budget to become very competent at making her own clothing decisions. Here's what Elyse shared with us:

Elyse's Story

Three years ago, when Katrina was fourteen, I started a clothing allowance. We went to the mall and I parked myself in the food court with a book and a cup of tea. Every thirty minutes or so, Katrina would come back with a progress report. After about three hours, she had a list of possible purchases from a variety of stores, and we went together to review them. I offered some comments, such as whether she could wear the white skirt she had picked out in the fall and how to tell whether the seams in a blouse were likely to come apart easily, but Katrina made the final decisions. Some decisions she regretted later, such as the expensive belt that she "had" to have and only wore twice, but she has generally made good decisions. I don't go with her anymore, but it's turned into a ritual that she brings home her purchases and shows them to me. She's had a clothing allowance now for three years, and I've seen her turn into a knowledgeable shopper who can tell the difference between good-quality and poor-quality merchandise.

Remember, too, that just because you give your child a clothing allowance doesn't mean you surrender your standards. Let your child know what type of clothing is and isn't acceptable. If your teenage daughter comes home with a string bikini and you don't approve, make her return it, and if she winds up with store credit where she doesn't like anything else, chalk it up to a learning experience.

THE ART OF SAVING AND CHECKING: HOW TO TEACH A PRESENT-ORIENTED KID TO THINK ABOUT THE FUTURE

Make sure to encourage your kids to save their unspent allowance money and use some of it for charity. If you choose to encourage them in this manner, increase their allowance by the amount you hope they'll save and use for charitable purposes. Though there's no right amount, 10 percent to 20 percent is popular with many parents with whom we work. Next, let's focus on how to encourage kids to save and why it helps them develop more than a healthy bank account.

Admittedly, it's difficult to get your six-year-old excited about saving money by explaining that if she deposits a dollar in a savings account that pays 2 percent annual interest, she'll have two dollars when she turns forty-two! Therefore, make the savings process more real and rewarding for your son or daughter. When your child is six or seven, take her to the bank and help her open a savings account. Match some portion of each deposit—for every five dollars she puts in, you put in five dollars—or make a "bonus deposit" to the account when your child's deposits reach certain "magic" numbers—twenty-five dollars, fifty dollars and so on. This will help create a more meaningful sum of money more quickly. At the same time, talk to your child about toys or other purchases she has her heart set on and write down the cost of each. By doing so, you create a target figure, one that gives your child a savings goal. This not only motivates her to save but creates a sense of achievement when the target figure is hit and the purchase is made.

If you have an older child, your goal should be to impress him with the power of compound interest. Not only will this help him grasp the benefits of placing money in an interest-bearing account, but it will drive home the benefits of long-term versus short-term thinking. Teenagers are so focused on the moment that they don't always understand the implications of their actions. For instance, they may fail to recognize how poor grades today might impact their happiness and success five or ten years down the road. If, however, they start saving, and compound interest provides them with a future sum that seems inconceivable in the present moment, they get a taste of why long-term thinking pays off.

Susan Beacham of Money Savvy Generation suggests that you ask your teens to record what they spend on things they want, every day for a week. They can even estimate at the end of each day what that dollar amount is. Typically these expenses are in the "I want" rather than the "I need" category: soda, chips, candy and cookies are the typical items listed. At the end of the week, sit down and see whether they have spent at least four dollars a day on "I wants." Chances are, they have spent that, and then some. As you review what was spent, ask them to quickly answer this multiple-choice test without using a calculator:

At age eighteen, you decide not to buy soda and snacks at the school cafeteria anymore. You save the four dollars per day. Every day, you put four dollars in a savings account at 2 percent annual interest and leave it alone. At age sixty-seven, your savings total is:

a) $1,159
b) $25,355
c) $71,540
d) $319,159

The answer is (d) $319,159. Note that $71,540 is from the daily deposits, and the remaining $247,619 is interest! Once you tell them the answer, or they realize it themselves, their eyes will widen with renewed respect for the power and importance of saving.

Many financially *un*intelligent parents open checking accounts for their kids, but they make the mistake of not doing much—or anything—with them. Financially intelligent parents, on the other hand, involve their children in managing the money in the account in creative ways.

One of the first mistakes to avoid is opening a checking account when your child is too young to learn from the experience. We know some children who were ready for a checking account when they were twelve, while others weren't ready for another four or five years. Determine your child's readiness by thinking about the following:

- *Is your child mathematical? Does she like playing with numbers, and does she do well at school in math classes?*
- *Does your child take his responsibilities seriously? Does he do his chores without you having to remind him, take care of a younger sibling, and the like?*
- *Is your child good with money in general? Does she have a grasp of what things cost and how to budget for things she wants?*

The more *yes* answers you have, the more likely your child is ready for a checking account.

When you open the account, you need to teach your child to reconcile the account monthly. Of course, there are parents who don't reconcile their own accounts, and if you're one of them, you need to change this particular behavior immediately. Invariably, this subject will come up when you're teaching your child to reconcile her account, and if you admit that you can't reconcile your own account, there's not much point in trying to teach her this money-management skill. If you need help in learning how to reconcile your checking account, there are several good resources available on the Internet: one is www.aboutchecking.com, which you can also use to help make learning financial concepts fun for teens who otherwise might get turned off by parental explanations. For younger children, a good source of information about the concept of checking accounts is www.kidsbank.com.

Reconciling balances isn't the point of this exercise. Rather, it's the opportunity to help your child be a thinking money manager. Just learning how to balance an account is no great shakes; you can balance your account and still practice irresponsible money-management behaviors. The balancing routine, however, gives your child the chance to reflect on her spending and saving decisions. With the benefit of hindsight, she can see the errors in judgment that might not have been apparent earlier. While it would be great if you could have discussions with your son or daughter right after they make a purchase, this is rarely possible. Plus, it's difficult for a teen to keep track of what she has been spending her allowance on when it's in cash. We know a few families where the children make sure they get receipts for everything they spend and go over the receipts with their parents every few weeks, but they tend to be the exceptions. For most kids, cash just tends to evaporate. When your child's allowance is deposited to her checking account, though, the canceled checks and bank statement provide a paper trail that you can discuss with her at the end of the month. When you review the bank statement and canceled checks with your teen, being judgmental just doesn't fly. Saying "I can't believe you spent thirty-five dollars for that teen idol's T-shirt" does not foster parent-child communication! Instead, try: "Are you happy you bought the T-shirt? Was it made well, and do you think you'll wear it a lot? Would you make the same decision again?" Steering the conversation that way is far more likely to generate a truly reflective response from your child.

GIVING YOUR CHILD CREDIT WHEN CREDIT IS DUE

The next step in helping your child learn to behave responsibly with money is to introduce him to plastic. We make this recommendation not because credit cards are wonderful but because they are everywhere, and we can no more ignore our child's need for credit card education than we can ignore his need for sex education. In 1998, John Simpson of Indiana University commented during an interview with the *Chicago Tribune*, "We lose more students to credit card debt than academic failure." The following year, sociologist Robert Manning commented in his book *Credit Card Nation*, "The unrestricted marketing of credit cards on college campuses is so aggressive that it now poses a greater threat than alcohol or sexually transmitted diseases." In 2004, the *Los Angeles Times* published an editorial by an outraged parent whose high school senior was being barraged at home with telephone calls offering credit cards that didn't need a parent's signature!

The Associated Press reported on June 24, 2004, that ten states—New York, Arkansas, California, Hawaii, Illinois, Louisiana, Missouri, New Mexico, Virginia and West Virginia—have either restricted the marketing of credit cards on campus or have required studies of credit card solicitation on campus. According to the Associated Press, 67 percent of college students now have at least one credit card, up from 43 percent in 1990. The average balance has ballooned from nine hundred dollars in 1990 to twenty-one hundred dollars today. It is not unheard of to find students with balances of twenty-five thousand dollars or more.

So, how do you practice financially intelligent behaviors when it comes to your kids and credit cards? Start with the equivalent of credit card training wheels: a debit card that is tied to your child's checking account. Remember that you are depositing your child's allowance into the checking account, and a debit card provides your child with an introduction to credit cards without the ability to overdraft. As an added bonus, your child will receive monthly checking account statements that show the debit card charges, yet another reason for financial management discussions between you and your child.

When your children are high school juniors and seniors, you can move them up to a preloaded credit card; this provides the experience of a real credit card without the possibility of getting into serious financial trouble. The Visa Buxx card, for instance, provides you with your child's credit card statement each month. Some parents are concerned that waiting a month to get the next statement is too long; they might consider obtaining a prepaid MasterCard through Net SpendCorp. (www.netspend.com), which allows users to sign up for an optional free service known as All-Access Alerts. Each time the card is used, a text message will be sent via e-mail to a computer or cell phone. All-Access Alerts provides you and your child with the ability to meet weekly (or even daily) to discuss credit card use. The downside of this type of service is that kids may feel that their parents are spying on them. Therefore, discuss the pros and cons of All-Access Alerts with your child. Don't sign up for it in secret. Whatever option you and your child choose, it will help prevent him from making credit card mistakes once he enters college.

Credit cards also give parents the opportunity to educate their children about the nature of credit. Though a preloaded credit card or a debit card tied to a checking account balance does not expose your children to interest payments, you can use the experience to talk about what happens when they have a real credit card. Read the credit card application and determine the annual percentage rate (APR). Explain how interest accrues and increases the cost of what is being purchased if the entire balance is not paid every month.

Here's an interesting "extra credit" exercise to do with an older adolescent. Ask her to imagine running up $2,500 on a credit card with a 19 percent annual interest rate. As part of this scenario, she makes only the required minimum monthly payment of 2 percent of the outstanding balance. Ask her to guess how long it will take to pay off the debt and how much interest she will pay in the process. The horrifying answers: 40.5 years and $8,098 in interest to finance the $2,500 purchase. The total cost of the purchase is actually $10,598, and she'll still be paying for it when she's fifty-seven years old!

RESPONSIBILITY COMES IN MANY FORMS: KEEP ALERT FOR MONEY-MANAGEMENT OPPORTUNITIES

We've focused the discussion here on the most common ways parents can help their children become financially responsible. In reality, you have a wide range of other options available to you. Here are three additional possibilities to consider:

- ***Job learning.*** *When your child is old enough, encourage him to find at least a part-time job during the summer. As we've discussed, this experience can help foster a work ethic. It also helps make your child more financially responsible, especially if he saves some of the money he earns to achieve a goal: college tuition, a car and so on. In many ways, retail positions where your child has to take money from customers is best. These jobs give him a bird's-eye view of the good and bad ways money is spent. Most kids who work in places such as clothing, electronics, grocery and toy stores are often aghast at what some people waste their money on as well as impressed by the savvy purchases others make. Your child may witness a grocery-store shopper who uses coupons so wisely that a significant part of her purchase each week is free. He may also witness people who spend money on merchandise that is shoddy or overpriced. Talk to your child about his observations, both positive and negative.*
- ***Investments.*** *The goal here isn't necessarily to make your child a savvy investor who is a master of hedge strategies before she leaves high school. Instead, it's to give her the chance to invest a small amount of her own money in a company and watch it grow or diminish. The key is to allow her to choose the company in which she believes and trusts. Maybe she loves her Apple computer or MP3 player. Suggest she do some research about the company online, and if she still wants to invest, help her do so. Allowing your child to gain ownership in a company confers a*

sense of responsibility. By her investment, she is putting her money where her heart is; she is saying that she believes enough in a given organization that she is willing to demonstrate this belief through action. Investing can help a child feel financially powerful and part of a larger world. Even a tiny amount of ownership can encourage her to take financial decisions seriously.

- ***Entrepreneurship****. From selling Girl Scout cookies and running lemonade stands to shoveling snow, mowing lawns and babysitting, kids have many entrepreneurial options. You can make your children aware of these options and nudge them in a given direction. Think about all the small, responsibility-building steps that come with the entrepreneurial territory. They have to make an argument for themselves as diligent and hardworking laborers; they need to set prices for their goods or services; they must make marketing decisions (Should they put up an ad on the bulletin board of the local supermarket? What kind of sign should they design for their lemonade stand?); they sometimes must take on partners and negotiate partnership shares of the profits. All these tasks foster fiscal responsibility.*

When Kevin was eight years old, he wanted a computer in his bedroom. His mother said that it wasn't in the budget but offered to match anything he earned. He started a neighborhood car-washing business that he called the BuBBles Company. He got some help producing advertising leaflets and soon had regular customers. One neighbor was so impressed that she bought him a DustBuster for his business so he could vacuum the upholstery. Within a few months he had earned enough that, with Mom's matching funds, he had the computer.

To help your kids maximize the learning involved in these experiences, talk to them about what they are doing. Most of the time, they'll be happy to relate stories about how babysitting the spoiled kid in the yellow house on the corner isn't worth the extra money his mom pays or how they set a new record for income by shoveling snow at ten homes in two hours. These discussions allow them to express their feelings about being responsible providers of goods and services and the rewards of and obstacles to being responsible.

Mary, a single mother and freelance writer, shared this story of her kids' first experience with entrepreneurship. She calls it "The Iced Tea Stand."

The Iced Tea Stand

My kids, who are eleven, twelve and thirteen, had been at each other's throats all morning. When they first asked me whether they could sell iced tea in the lobby of our apartment building I responded with a resounding no. The whole idea conjured up visions of stern letters from the building management . . . but I had work to do and relented after some negotiations, telling them that while they could dip into the family supply of instant iced tea and take a few paper cups and a tray or two of ice, after that they were on their own. I also told them to set up their stand outside just in front of the building, figuring the City of New York would go easier on them than the co-op board.

I retreated to my office to work and was only dimly aware of occasional kitchen commotion. After about an hour I stepped out and ran smack into my middle son, Henry, who was looking for a pitcher in which to haul more water downstairs. I decided it was time to go investigate.

The kids had set up their stand, consisting of two TV snack tables side by side, in front of our building in plain view of the doorman, who appeared to be both amused and impressed by the enterprise. It was a hot spring day, and there were plenty of families strolling by on their way to Central Park, as well as neighborhood regulars on their way to shopping and running errands. People driving down the street were also attracted and were pulling up to purchase drinks.

The kids had also rigged up an umbrella over the stand to keep it shaded. They had made hand-lettered signs, and business was so brisk they had already replaced the initial supply of cups and ice out of their gross profits, dispatching Jeremy, the oldest, to the corner deli. Their cooperative spirit was unlike any I'd seen for months.

"We're getting lots of business because we're only charging twenty-five cents a cup," my daughter, Elise, told me, jangling a shoebox full of quarters at me. "And we're offering free cups of water and free samples of tea to everyone who stops by," Henry added. "Then they come back and buy from us because we've been nice to them." I immediately flashed on my Marketing 101 class and told the kids they were doing exactly what they needed to do to be successful: They had a good product in a visible place, their pricing was right and they were promoting it well. (They were also exercising a fifth P of marketing—politeness, thanking every customer after each sale, to my delight.)

At four o'clock I asked them to shut down operations for the afternoon, clean up and bring all their money upstairs. We all pulled out pencil and paper and figured out how much they had made, how much it had cost in supplies (including three slices of pizza at lunchtime and ice cream in the midafternoon). Each child had made exactly $4.91—which they were thrilled with.

Answer to Financially Intelligent Brainteaser

If your son were your employee, A would be the correct answer; you'd give him an increase in pay for an increase in responsibilities. Treating a child like an employee who works for money, however, is not what a financially intelligent parent does. Similarly, allowing him to shirk a family responsibility (answer B) such as mowing the lawn in exchange for other labor sends a negative message—you're telling him that you think he can handle only a relatively small amount of responsibility. Answer C is also a mistake, in that you are disrespecting his time and effort; you want to help him make the connection between doing extra work and receiving rewards for this extra effort. The correct answer, D, maintains the separation between routine chores and allowances. Setting up special payments for special chores communicates that these chores are outside the area of routine family responsibility. ◆

9

SPEND TIME AND MONEY IN WAYS THAT ARE CONSISTENT WITH YOUR VALUES

Financially Intelligent Brainteaser

You just received a call from an executive recruiter offering you a job that would more than double your salary. It would mean uprooting you, your spouse and your two elementary-school-age children from a city where you're all very happy, and moving to a third world country. In addition, your prospective employer expects you to work extremely long hours for the next three years and do a great deal of traveling. Though you're not particularly excited about the company you'd be joining or even the job itself, you are attracted by the salary and the possibility that having the position on your resume might lead to other great jobs.

What should your decision be?

A. Accept the job because you could probably double your savings in three years since there won't be any place to spend money.
B. Accept the job because it not only pays well but it may ultimately lead to a better job.
C. Accept the job because you and your spouse value diversity, and living in a third world country will expose your children to a more diverse culture than they've ever experienced.
D. Reject the job because it goes against your belief that family comes first.

(Answer at end of chapter)

As an experiment, see which of the following questions your child can answer about what you've been doing recently:

- *What did I watch on television last weekend?*
- *What did I say was my favorite meal for dinner last week?*
- *With whom did I have a long phone conversation the other night?*
- *What book am I currently reading?*
- *When we went shopping last week, what did I buy?*

Most children are much better able to answer the last question than the other four. Though you may not be aware of it, your children watch your spending habits like hawks. No matter what their ages, they are tuned in to your purchasing decisions. This is tremendously significant because the ways you spend money communicate your values. Financially intelligent parents are highly conscious of their spending decisions and the values that are being communicated. They learn to be conscious about these behaviors so they can communicate the right values to their children.

Similarly, financially intelligent parents are vigilant about how they spend their time. Parents who are workaholics or who devote excessive amounts of free time to making or monitoring their money (day trading, reading nothing but get-rich-quick books, etc.) are essentially telling their children that they value money over family. Please understand that we're not suggesting that you become antimaterialistic or lower your career aspirations. The key word is *excessive*. When you miss numerous opportunities to talk with your kids, take them to the zoo and go with them on vacations because you're always too busy making money, you're practicing financially *un*intelligent behaviors.

Being aware of and managing how we spend our time and money are trickier than they might seem; we may think these behaviors are sending our kids the right messages, but excessive behaviors do not.

Money makes us do strange things, and sometimes without our knowing it, our money behaviors fly in the face of our family values. Let's examine how the gap between our behaviors and our communicated values affects our kids.

BALANCING MONEY AND MEANING

Joe Dominguez, author of *Your Money or Your Life,* refers to time as hours of "life energy" and treats time spent on earning a living as "maintenance." If you are thirty-five years old, Dominguez figures that you have about 365,000 hours of remaining life energy ahead of you. As parents, we need to decide how many of those hours we are going to spend making a living and how many we are going to spend having a life. If we want to have a life, we have to control the role that money plays rather than letting money control us. As parents, we sometimes must choose between time and money. Say you want to buy a tennis club membership for yourself that costs twenty-five hundred dollars, and your family income is eighty thousand dollars a year. After taxes and social security, you have to work about two weeks to earn enough for the membership. If you join the tennis club, you'll have to economize on this year's family vacation. So you need to ask yourself whether it's more important to join the tennis club or have a nicer family vacation.

You may not think a decision to join the tennis club will have an adverse impact on your kids, and you may be right. If, however, you make ten or twenty similar decisions over the course of a year, your children will get the message: You don't place a particularly high value on family. Obviously, this isn't your intent, but it's still the message that is sent. The goal, therefore, is to make conscious choices about how you spend your time and money. While no one always chooses to spend time and money on others rather than themselves, financially intelligent parents find a good balance in their choices. They don't inadvertently teach the wrong values to their kids.

As much as we may want to convey good values to our children, something may get lost in the translation from intention to action. For instance, we know two financially intelligent parents, Maureen and Barry, who had read our earlier book and were trying to put its lessons into practice. One Saturday morning Maureen took their eldest daughter, Haley, to the local mall to buy a new dress, shoes and a purse for a special family wedding. That afternoon, Haley went with Barry to the local hardware store for batteries. Haley subsequently commented that she had a better time with her father than with her mother. Maureen couldn't believe that an eleven-year-old girl would prefer buying batteries for the house than a dress for herself. Haley, though, explained that what was important to her wasn't what they were buying. She didn't like that Maureen rushed through the morning in order to get home in time to take her other two kids to their activities. Barry, on the other hand, wasn't in a hurry, so Haley had more connecting time with her father. Maureen realized that her hurried approach negated the family value of enjoying an experience together, that Haley needed to feel that her mom was truly present more than she needed to go shopping for new clothes.

As role models, we are communicating money values to our children even when we're not talking to them. According to Albert Mehrabian, PhD, a pioneer in the field of nonverbal communication (body language), the majority of communication takes places through such nonverbal channels as gesture, posture, tone of voice and facial expression. How we tip and treat service employees, for instance, contains value messages that kids pick up on. If someone does a good job and you are impolite and leave an insufficient tip, your behavior communicates that you don't care very much about other people; plus, you're using money (the tip) to devalue another human being. There's nothing wrong about leaving no tip at all if the server generally does a poor job. This is an opportunity to share values with your kids: "We leave tips to thank the server for a good job; this server didn't do a good job, so I'm not leaving a tip" (or "I'm leaving a smaller tip").

Your moods around money issues, too, can send unintended messages about values to your kids, as Amy and Richard discovered. Amy, an interior decorator, and Richard, a midlevel manager with a national company, are the parents of twins, Samantha and Kimberly, who turned out to be talented musicians—Samantha was a singer and Kimberly was a pianist. When the girls were nine, Amy and Richard decided to buy their dream house. Buying the new house would be a bit of a financial stretch, but Richard was in line for a promotion and they would live only five minutes from the twins' private school. They used their credit cards to help furnish the house. Richard's expected promotion, though, didn't come through. Even with two incomes, they didn't have enough to pay the mortgage, pay down the credit cards, keep their daughters in private school and pay for music lessons. They either had to sell their dream house and try to find something cheaper or keep the dream house and economize by sending the twins to public school and stopping the music lessons. While they were trying to make this decision, Amy and Richard displayed a great deal of anxiety and were angrier (at both each other and the twins) than normal. In the end, it didn't matter which decision Amy and Richard made; the anxiety generated by money was obvious to Kimberly and Samantha. People are very complex, and each of us processes information differently. One of the twins might respond to the experience by viewing money as something to be avoided while the other might lean in the other direction and strive to fill her life with money to avoid these negative feelings.

Sometimes we send more subtle emotional signals related to money that still affect our kids in significant ways. Even though we don't believe that money provides true emotional satisfaction and fulfillment, we might use money to buy things because we're depressed. When we're depressed we tend to feel empty. We experience a need to fill this sense of emptiness. Even if we value frugality, we're likely to think subconsciously: *I am empty. I need to fill myself up with things because I'm not enough by myself, so I'll go buy x, y or z and I'll feel better.* Buying things to help depression is a quick fix that doesn't last. In fact, it may make us feel more depressed than before because we come to realize that we are spending money in a futile effort to make ourselves feel better. This is a classic example of money behaviors being in conflict with our values. More significantly, we are modeling the wrong value for our kids. We're essentially communicating that money can buy happiness.

While financially intelligent parents are as likely to get depressed or be angry as anyone else, they are aware that regularly tying these emotions to money issues conveys the wrong messages to their kids. They are especially alert for situations like the one that Amy and Richard faced, and make an extra effort to shield their children from the anxiety or other potential negative emotions that might surround a major money decision.

MAKING THE DAILY CONNECTION

While you won't regularly encounter extreme situations like the one Amy and Richard had to deal with, you will find opportunities surfacing daily to send value-positive messages to your kids. You can connect money behaviors with good values through word and deed, an absolutely essential task given the peer-group pressure your kids are encountering as they grow up.

Your child is highly motivated to conform to his peer group's values rather than yours, especially when he is an adolescent. Teenagers try to establish an identity separate from their parents' by conforming to the standards of their peer group: *In order to show adults—especially my parents—my disdain for the way they all dress the same way, like the same boring movies and listen to the same boring music, I'm going to assert my individuality by dressing the same way as my friends, going to the same movies as my friends and listening to the same music as my friends.* Often, the values of the peer group do not include making wise spending decisions, saving money or contributing to charity. As a result, your children could become overly materialistic. It's also possible that they will come to believe that when they feel depressed, spending money can make them feel better.

We can avoid these negative consequences if we start helping our kids connect money and values long before adolescence. For instance, one parent seized the opportunity to talk about money and values when her six-year-old tried to deceive the tooth fairy. When six-year-old Maggie lost her first tooth, her mother bought her a tooth fairy pillow with a special pocket in it for the tooth. She explained that losing your first tooth is very special and that the tooth fairy was going to leave Maggie five dollars, but for the rest of her teeth, Maggie was going to receive just one dollar each. Maggie thought this was a great idea because she was getting interested in money. She had just started receiving a three-dollar-a-week allowance that she tended to spend at the local arts and crafts store to buy herself supplies to make things. Leaving a tooth for the tooth fairy was a great way to be able to buy additional stickers and supplies. When Maggie lost her second tooth, she put the tooth in the pocket together with a note asking the tooth fairy to leave her tooth behind. Sure enough, the next morning both the tooth and a dollar bill were in the pocket. The next night Maggie's mom noticed that Maggie was sleeping with the tooth fairy pillow again. When she asked why, they had the following conversation:

MAGGIE: I'm going to get more money, Mommy. I put my tooth back in the pillow.

MOMMY: *You can't do that. You can't fool the tooth fairy like that.*

MAGGIE: Yes, I can. I'll sleep with my mouth closed!

MOMMY: *No, you can't do that. It's not right to fool the tooth fairy like that. You're not being truthful in the way you're getting money. If you want an opportunity to make some more money, tell Mommy or Daddy and we'll see if we can find something extra for you to do around the house.*

Connecting money and values is something every financially intelligent parent can do using a variety of tools and techniques. First and foremost, make a commitment to spend as much time as possible with your family so your kids see you're more than a money-making machine. Beyond that, here are some other approaches you might find useful:

Articulate a Money-Values Vocabulary. Neurologists tell us that thinking is unconscious. While we don't remember the actual thoughts, we do remember the words that accompany our thoughts. That's why it's so important to give your kids a money-values vocabulary. This means having the words to make money decisions based on their values. For instance, you walk into a store, see a beautiful coat and reflexively want to buy it, but then you say to yourself, *I'm not going to buy it because I believe in moderation, and the price of the coat isn't moderate.* Kids, too, need this type of values-focused language when they're dealing with money issues.

Elisabeth Guthrie, MD, the clinical director of the Learning Diagnostic Center at Blythedale Children's Hospital in Valhalla, New York, and the coauthor of *The Trouble with Perfect*, observes that parents can learn a lot about the importance of teaching kids values by watching swimmers in a pool. Swimmers need to push off against the end wall of the pool in order to make the best possible turn. When it comes to values, we parents need to be the wall our kids push against, and part of being the wall is giving our kids a money-values vocabulary. When they are trying to decide whether to spend their entire allowance on video games, like their friends do, their money-values vocabulary can help them resist peer-group pressure. They can say to themselves, *I believe in saving at least some of my money for more important things in the future, so it doesn't make sense to spend all of it each week on these games.*

Teaching kids this vocabulary isn't as difficult as it sounds. The problem is that most parents keep their values in their heads rather than articulating them consistently. Make a conscious effort to verbalize your values related to the use, management and acquisition of money. Here are some examples of ways to articulate these values:

> *"I will treasure the memories of our family trip to Europe. I'm glad we spent the money to stay an extra day."*
>
> *"It was really important for me to change jobs, even though I had to take a pay cut; I feel like I found my true calling."*
>
> *"We had to make some sacrifices when we were younger to afford the house, but we're glad we did."*
>
> *"It's important to keep track of what you spend on the school trip and stay within your budget."*

The above statements endorse family values, meaningful work, long-term planning and responsibility. They clearly make the connections among actions, money and values. You can supplement these value-connecting statements with similar types of questions. For instance, you can ask your kids the following:

> *"Will you use it or do you just want it?"*
>
> *"Is it really important to you?"*
>
> *"Do you think you might quickly get tired of that toy you're considering buying?"*
>
> *"Do you think there might be better ways to use some of your money?"*
>
> *"If you balance your checkbook weekly, will you feel more in control of your financial situation?"*

A third technique is simply saying no and explaining why in value-based terms. For instance, thirteen-year-old Brian announced to his parents, Leah and Jerry, that they "had" to get a really cool eight-thousand-dollar, fifty-inch flat-screen television just like the one his cousin Ian's family had bought that week. "The store is offering zero percent financing for five years," said Brian. "I did the math, and it will only cost about a hundred and thirty dollars a month." Leah and Jerry could have copped out by simply saying, "We can't afford it" or "We don't have the money." Instead, they told their son, "It's very nice, but spending that much money on a TV isn't something we want to do as a family. We're saving for college, and we think that putting money away for education is more important."

Other ways of communicating a values-based *no* include:

> *"Yes, Grandma's offer of a car was very generous, but we think you should earn at least some of the money necessary to buy a car."*

> *"Other families have different values. This is the way our family does things."*

> *"We don't want to buy from that company. They have a bad record of using child labor."*

Help Your Children Understand the Difference Between Using Money for Self-Worth and Using Money for Self-Fulfillment. In all the years we have worked with families, not once have we seen anyone ruined by too much or too little money. The problem isn't money; it's money without values. Neither being rich nor struggling to make ends meet is an obstacle to leading a meaningful, happy life. On the other hand, we've seen people who have ruined their lives because they've defined themselves by money; they have equated the amount of money in their bank account with their worth as human beings; they have viewed their vacations, cars and homes as life measures. Money becomes nothing more than a scorecard: "I am my money; therefore, the more money I have, the more I am; the less money I have, the less I am."

While we hope none of you have this attitude about money, many parents do define themselves to some extent by how they spend their money. As a result, their children become confused between self-worth and self-fulfillment. Kids who grow up confusing their self-worth with their net worth don't learn to incorporate the value of *enough* into their money vocabulary. It's natural to want to be a better person, and if you've taught your child that money equals self-worth, it's natural for your child to want more money. The problem is that this type of thinking can result in your kids growing up to become workaholics or the type of superficial people who spend money to impress others. Walter, married and with two preteen children, became interested in golf and signed up for lessons at the local golf course. For the first few lessons, Walter used clubs provided by the golf pro. Walter's brother-in-law, though, loved golf and had expensive golf clubs. Within a month, Walter "needed" better clubs. He spent thousands of dollars on custom-made titanium and graphite clubs and the finest possible bag. Within ninety days, Walter decided that golf was boring and stopped playing altogether. Walter had spent a great deal of money as well as time on an activity that was ultimately meaningless. His children, who observed these events unfolding, were taught that it's okay to spend money without much thought.

Don't be like Walter. Instead, teach your children that money is a tool, not an end in and of itself. To teach this lesson effectively, consider this set of values-consistent behaviors:

Guard Against Excess. People often disagree over what is excessive because the term is so subjective. We think of excess in terms of motivation—why you are spending the money—and the message that your behavior is sending your kids. Even though you can afford to spend the money, your motivation combined with your behavior may be sending your kids the wrong message. For example, if you are just learning how to play golf, don't start off buying an expensive set of clubs; buy or rent a decent but inexpensive set while you're learning, and then consider investing in a more expensive set after a number of months of playing and loving the game. Your behavior tells the kids that it's important not to spend money until you're sure it's a good idea. If you need a new car and can afford to buy a Mercedes, buying one isn't excess. But if you trade in a perfectly good car on a Mercedes because your business partner just bought one, you're sending your kids the message that it's important to keep up with the Joneses. If you throw an elaborate birthday party for your five-year-old in order to top the party thrown by a neighbor for his kid, your motives and your behavior are sending the wrong message.

Don't Brag Incessantly That Your Car, House, Boat, Vacation Home, Bike or Other Object Is "the Best." Treating your purchases as meaningful accomplishments creates values confusion in kids. Of course, we all have a tendency to brag about getting great deals on cars or other high-ticket items, and doing so occasionally won't do any harm. It's only when you talk constantly about your "things" that you are likely to confuse self-worth with self-fulfillment.

Allow Your Children to See How You Really Measure Self-Worth. Saving money to spend on a great family vacation or being able to provide for a college education are real accomplishments. Similarly, working at a job you love or spending time with close friends also conveys what you consider important in life. Share with your kids that these are important aspects of your life. Let them know that this is how you measure your life rather than by how much money you make or how many things you buy.

In other words, live your values, and let your kids see you living them. If you are looking for a role model of a parent living his values, try filmmaker Steven Spielberg. Spielberg strongly believes in the importance of education and wanted his kids to go to college. In 1968, though, he had dropped out of California State University–Long Beach to become a filmmaker. Thirty-four years later, he went back to college and accumulated enough credits to graduate from the College of the Arts with a bachelor's degree in 2002. (Like many people who go back to college in their forties and fifties, Spielberg was given credit for some life experience. The advanced filmmaking class required students to produce a twelve-minute film. Sharyn Blumenthal, director of the Film and Electronic Arts Department, told the *Los Angeles Times* that the professors gave Spielberg credit for *Schindler's List,* which earned him Oscars for best director and best film, even though it exceeded the twelve-minute limit!) Upon graduating, Spielberg described his decision to complete his studies as "a personal note for my own family" and as a message to young people everywhere about the importance of education. He added, "How could I tell my kids to go to college when I had not graduated?"

Use Words and Deeds to Communicate Values When Shopping with Your Kids. Stores are laboratories for learning money-related values, especially before your children reach adolescence. What you buy and what you say about the products you see can have a huge impact on your kids. Being in a retail environment motivates kids to pay closer attention to what you say and do. When you point out that an advertised toy is shoddily constructed, as in the story of the James Bond briefcase in chapter 5, or that a snack-food label indicates that it contains huge amounts of fat or sodium, your comments are much more likely to resonate with the values beneath the surface. Not only might your kids be interested in a particular product you're talking about, but they're in an environment that causes them to think about what you're doing or saying. In a store, they are surrounded by thousands of products—this is a buying and selling landscape that causes them to think more deeply about spending behaviors. When they accompany you to purchase the antibiotic for their ear infection and you tell the pharmacist you want the generic rather than the name brand, your child will understand that you value responsible spending. When you point out the trick of positioning impulse items next to the checkout register in supermarkets, they'll understand that you value thinking before acting.

Try to take your children to smaller, privately owned (as opposed to big chain) stores. For years, Susan has been taking her children shopping for books at Dutton's, one of the few privately owned bookstores in Los Angeles. Owner Doug Dutton provides personalized services, and as Susan says, "The employees are like knowledgeable librarians who have actually read the books. They seem to love what they're doing." Her sons' eyes light up when they get Dutton's gift certificates as birthday and Christmas gifts, and the boys are eager to go and peruse the shelves for their picks. Susan is creating meaningful rituals, which kids of all ages enjoy. She's also teaching her kids such values as loyalty and the importance of individuality.

Here are some basic actions you can take while shopping and the values they communicate:

Action: **Reject products that seem poorly made.**

Value: *Quality*

Action: **Talk about what you consider to be a good deal and why.**

Value: *Analytical thinking*

Action: **Tell your kids when you think a toy or other type of product is especially well designed or conceptualized.**

Value: *Creativity*

Action: **Make judgments about products you feel are particularly beneficial or particularly worthless (you might praise organic cereal makers and criticize manufacturers that exploit foreign workforces, for instance).**

Value: *A sense of right and wrong*

Action: **Buy household supplies in bulk at membership warehouse stores such as Costco or Sam's Club.**

Value: *Careful planning and careful shopping*

Many other options exist for parents who take their kids shopping and want to use these experiences to illustrate their values. Think of stores, including online retailers, as environments filled with opportunities to teach your children about money and values. Expose your child to a range of shopping experiences when he's young. Go to outlet malls, boutiques and chains; visit Amazon.com as well as a small, specialty children's bookstore. After an initial round of visits, you can frequent the type of stores that represent your values, but you want to give your child a sense of the choices out there. You want your sons and daughters to be astute shoppers, and by exposing them to a diversity of experiences, you're communicating that you value informed decision making. They may choose to be Wal-Mart shoppers or to patronize only the most exclusive shops, but they will make their choices with full awareness of what is available to them.

BEWARE THE DANGERS OF RATIONALIZING HOW YOU SPEND MONEY

Sometimes it is difficult to determine whether money decisions really communicate values to our kids or are just rationalizations for our selfish behaviors. Remember Brian, who wanted his parents, Leah and Jerry, to purchase an eight-thousand-dollar giant-screen television just like the one his cousin Ian's family had bought? Although they eventually said no, Leah and Jerry didn't dismiss Brian's request out of hand. They discussed how they really wanted to spend more time with Brian, how they could rent movies and watch them together and how the giant television would help them achieve this goal. When Leah pointed out that they could achieve this same goal with their current smaller television, they realized that they were rationalizing the purchase of a television by telling themselves it would communicate how much they valued family togetherness. They, like their son, thought the giant television was cool. That was fine, but they were smart enough not to fool themselves into thinking that purchasing it would help convey their values.

Here are some other examples of parents who rationalize their spending decisions:

- *They purchase a million-dollar home for status reasons. They tell their kids that they bought the home because the area schools are good and they value education.*

- *They don't like spending money, so they send their children to a cheap summer camp that offers few opportunities for growth even though they can afford to send them to a better camp with many more activities. They tell their kids that they selected the cheap camp so they can experience diversity.*

- *They purchase an eco-friendly hybrid car because it is trendy. They tell the kids they bought it because they value the environment.*

Most of us can spot these rationalizations if we are honest about our motivations for a purchase. Avoid using rationalizations to justify spending money when you talk to your kids. Kids are pretty good at seeing through rationalizations and may view you as a hypocrite. They may also start perceiving even sincere attempts to communicate values as suspect and never reap the benefit of the values they are designed to convey.

Answer to Financially Intelligent Brainteaser

Answer D is correct because it gives parents a chance to make choices that benefit the entire family. It is a difficult choice, but these difficult choices are exactly the ones that make an impression on kids. They tell children unequivocally that a parent values family more than money. The first three answers are rationalizations of one type or another; they may sound convincing to an outsider, but the children will know their dad chose the money over them. This doesn't mean that parents should never take jobs that give them opportunities to advance their careers; some decisions about jobs occupy gray areas where there is no right answer. In this instance, however, it was a clear choice between spending more time with family or dislocating the family in pursuit of more money. ◆

10

BE AWARE OF AND MODERATE YOUR EXTREME MONEY TENDENCIES

Financially Intelligent Brainteaser

You love to shop, and because you and your spouse have been doing well in your careers, you've been able to indulge this habit more in the past few years than you ever could before. You've noticed, though, that your elementary-school-age children aren't particularly happy when you go off on weekend or weeknight shopping expeditions. Your younger daughter, especially, seems resentful of the time you devote to shopping and sulks both before you leave and when you return. Your older son doesn't sulk, but he regularly makes snide references about how "shopping is your life." Though you know that shopping has begun to take a disproportionate amount of your free time, you justify it as a harmless diversion, telling yourself, "Some people play golf, some people work out; I shop for fun." Still, you worry that all the shopping you do might be having a negative effect on your kids.

To counter this effect, what might you do?

A. Insist your children join you on more of your shopping trips, turning the experience into family time and helping them become educated shoppers.
B. Make sure that when you return from shopping you bring your kids presents to show that you were thinking of them.
C. Limit the amount of time you spend shopping and try to find other activities to do for fun.
D. Go cold turkey and stop shopping altogether.

(Answer at end of chapter)

Money, as we have pointed out, is an excellent servant but a terrible master. When money becomes your master, your attitudes and actions are likely to fall in the extreme range. Your tendency to be frugal can turn into miserly behavior or your casual money management can become chaotic. Essentially, your money tendency can evolve into a money disorder. These extreme tendencies get you and your family into trouble or cause you and your family a great deal of concern and grief. Incurring so much credit card debt that you have to sell your house and move to an apartment in a cheaper neighborhood is one example. Another is thinking you never have enough money so you become a workaholic, spending six or seven days a week in the office and feeling guilty when you're home with your family. Divorce, bankruptcy and criminal convictions are all possible consequences of money disorders.

Most of you, though, probably won't encounter these dire consequences. Nonetheless, you can still be hurting your children if your attitudes and actions in any money area are over the top. The more "abnormal" you are in terms of money use, acquisition or management, the more negative the impact on your kids. Financially intelligent parents may exhibit extreme money behavior on occasion, but they learn to recognize and moderate it. To that end, let's start out by examining the range of money disorders and how they disrupt families.

101 VARIETIES OF DISORDER

Money disorders have been around for a long time. For at least twenty-six hundred years, we have been passing laws in a futile attempt to regulate how people use their money. In 594 BC, Athens enacted the first of what are known as *sumptuary laws*, for the purpose of curbing "conspicuous consumption" and encouraging "public morality." During the reign of Queen Elizabeth I, Parliament passed similar laws in an attempt to limit the way both men and women dressed—to "curb extravagance, protect fortunes, and make clear the necessary and appropriate distinctions between levels of society." After all, if you couldn't tell a servant from a princess at a glance, the very fabric of Elizabethan English society might unravel! The United States has not been exempt from attempts to regulate money behavior. Most of the colonies passed sumptuary laws. As late as 1880, the issue was so prominent that the platform of the Democratic Party declared itself opposed to sumptuary laws. Of course, human nature being what it is, sumptuary laws have been impossible to enforce and people have continued to allow money to be their master.

We could spend an entire book listing variations on the extreme money behavior theme. For our purposes here, though, let's spotlight the more common varieties of extreme money behavior:

- ***Shop till you drop.*** *Some people shop not because they need to buy specific items but as a way of dealing with other problems in their lives. Just as some individuals use food as a temporary balm for what ails them, shopping addicts use malls, consumer electronics stores and boutiques in the same way. This behavior becomes extreme when it takes up significant amounts of time each week and when purchases are often random or even unnecessary. Kids see their parents buying things almost as a reflex. Though they wouldn't articulate it in this way, children grasp that parents are using shopping as a coping mechanism. Spending money to deal with deeper emotional issues is not a good lesson to teach children.*

- ***Pay cash for everything.*** *This individual refuses to use a credit card or get a bank loan. He despises debt of any sort and will sacrifice his own and his family's comfort and happiness to avoid the psychological burden of owing money. While it's financially prudent to avoid a lot of debt, it's financially unintelligent to avoid it at all costs. Some people deny their family a decent home, a safe car and access to good schools because they would need a loan to make these things possible. Kids observe smaller manifestations of this extreme money attitude, from arguing with* *a spouse about this cash-only policy to refusing to buy things in stores when there isn't cash on hand. Debt, then, becomes a nightmare in the eyes of children—even an outstanding balance of a few hundred dollars on a credit card looms as a disaster.*

- ***Agonize over unbalanced checking accounts.*** *Everyone should balance his or her checking account and teach this skill to the kids, but no one should rant and rave when the account doesn't balance to the penny. When this type of extreme behavior is repeated on a number of occasions, kids may come to loathe any type of money-management requirement or they may become as compulsive about it as their parent.*

- ***Fret over going to the poorhouse.*** *It's fine to be consciously frugal. But some parents see financial ruin around every corner. Every expenditure is a cause for alarm. Unlike some others with extreme money behaviors, these people spend money, but they can't spend it without complaining about what the expenditure might mean for their future. In a kid's mind, spending money becomes associated with catastrophic results.*

- ***Rack up mammoth credit card debt.*** *There are mothers and fathers who use credit cards as if they were never going to be asked to pay at the end of the month. Kids see parents whipping out credit cards at every purchasing opportunity, fostering the illusion that everything is affordable. Then the unpaid balance becomes so enormous that their parents can no longer use their credit cards. Suddenly (or so it seems from a child's perspective), nothing is affordable. This change is tremendously confusing for children, and it may foster dysfunctional money behaviors when they become adults—they are averse to buying anything on credit or they go on the same credit card binges that their parents did.*

- ***Act as if money can buy love.*** *Parents who travel a lot may feel guilty about their absences and attempt to compensate by lavishing gifts (rather than attention) on their children. Other people grew* *up in homes where they were given very little by their parents, and they compensate by giving their own kids too much. While it is normal to display love by giving someone a present, it becomes abnormal when gifts and other financial expenditures become a substitute for love. Giving kids more than they want or need doesn't just foster a sense of entitlement and produce spoiled kids, but can cause self-esteem problems. When parents attempt to buy love, they are telling their children that they would rather give them their money than their time. These kids can grow up feeling worthless.*

Other variations on these themes include:

- *refusing to give one penny to charities, homeless people and others in need, and never volunteering to help others*
- *spending almost every waking, nonwork hour concentrating on making money by day trading, reading articles and books about investing, visiting Web sites related to investing and so on*
- *becoming sullen or even depressed over relatively minor financial setbacks, such as not receiving a raise at work, having to pay an unexpected car repair bill or receiving an insurance premium increase*
- *fighting frequently with your spouse over money issues, such as spending money on clothes, food, vacations, being a bad manager of household finances, giving the children too much or too little money, being a miser or a spendthrift "just like your mom" (or dad) and not earning enough money*
- *nagging family members constantly for "extravagance" even though the expenditures are relatively minor and the family can easily afford them*
- *acting like you have less money than you actually do and using this behavior as an excuse not to take vacations, provide children with music lessons or go out to eat*

No matter what the extreme behavior might be, the most common effect on kids can be causing them to question their own self-worth: "If I were a better person, my parents would get braces for my teeth / not spend every weekend in the office / not feel they have to break the law to make money to buy me things / let me take piano lessons / not make me buy all of my clothes at the secondhand store." You may not realize it, but children are quick to blame themselves for their parents' extremely bad money habits. They look at their parents' compulsive money management and think, "My mom is so worried about accounting for every penny because she wants to have enough to buy me all the things I want; I'm too greedy." Kids experience real injury to the self when parents withhold money unreasonably. They have no sense of being given to, emotionally or materially, and this type of parental money behavior can result in children growing up to be either overspenders or extremely frugal, believing that they don't deserve anything.

On the other extreme, overindulgent parents create injury to a child's self in another way. If you can't say *no* and *enough* to your kids and you give them everything they want, you are doing the equivalent of *overpraising* your child. While positive reinforcement is great, too much praise diminishes the meaning of what you are saying. Your child becomes accustomed to the praise and its value is reduced. Kids who are consistently overpraised often learn to exhibit narcissistic, entitled behavior. So do kids who get everything they want as soon as they ask for it. Overindulgent parents also fail to give kids structure in their lives. Kids need structure. In studies of overindulged children, both boys and girls routinely tell researchers that they see themselves as not being loved and valued enough for their parents to spend the necessary time and effort to help them learn boundaries and limits. Children who are given everything they want as soon as they want it begin to lose faith in themselves.

WORST-CASE SCENARIOS

At best, extreme behaviors expose children to parents who act neurotically around money. At worst, they expose them to moms and dads who break laws, declare bankruptcy and disrupt normal family functioning in all sorts of ways. We'd like to relate a few stories as cautionary tales.

Betsy and Curt had been married twelve years and had a seven-year-old daughter, Nina. When Betsy was a child, she saw her mother changing price tags on furniture at antique shops in order to "get things cheaper." Betsy, though, exhibited money behaviors in the normal range until Curt lost his job and the family had to downsize their standard of living. Betsy quickly sunk into a depression and dealt with her dark feelings by shoplifting cosmetics and other small items. Unlike her mother, Betsy was caught. The family spent much of their remaining savings on lawyer and psychiatrist bills. Therapy helped Betsy deal with her depression, but the family was left with no savings, no annual family vacation and a mother with an arrest record. Though it is still too early to know what effect this extreme behavior will have on Nina, the odds are that it will be significant. Nina witnessed two shoplifting episodes, including the one where Betsy was caught and arrested. She also was acutely aware of her mother's black moods after Curt lost his job. For Nina, money has acquired a power far beyond an exchange medium. It has the power to make her mother steal and to cause her to be depressed. If Nina doesn't deal with these issues as she becomes older, she could end up as the third generation in her family to exhibit extreme money behaviors.

Ryan and Joyce were married eight years and had two children, ages three and six, when Ryan's money issues began causing problems. Ryan always had a need to keep up with the Joneses, and when the family remodeled their kitchen and family room, they maxed out their credit cards buying the finest appliances and furniture. Ryan commented, "Saying no makes me feel poor." Though Ryan had a good job that paid him almost one hundred thousand dollars annually, he and Joyce used credit as if Ryan made twice that amount. In the past, both Ryan and Joyce were able to rationalize their credit sprees with phrases such as "You only go round once in life" and "I could get hit by a bus tomorrow." This time, though, they really charged too much. When they started falling behind in their bill payments, Joyce became alarmed, but Ryan was in full-fledged denial. He was convinced that the credit card companies would cut him some slack, that he could use his expected end-of-year bonus to make additional payments and that if worse came to worst, he could always get another job that paid more than the one he had. Of course, what actually happened was that they seriously damaged their credit rating, and two credit card companies turned their accounts over to collection agencies. The anxiety level in their house was extremely high, and Ryan responded to it by being short-tempered, while Joyce was quietly morose. Joyce, who used to take the kids on outings all the time, suddenly stopped doing anything, afraid of spending one more penny than she had to. Ryan barked at his children for the slightest misbehavior, and he and Joyce had a number of fights when Ryan used a small inheritance to buy a new car (he justified it to Joyce by saying that things had been rather dismal in their household over the past year and they all needed something to cheer them up). Their children clearly were confused by and resented their parents' new attitudes and actions. They didn't understand why they could no longer afford the great vacations and outings they used to enjoy. They also were concerned by the continuous anxiety in their household as well as the parental fights and their parents' bad moods. Ryan and Joyce finally had to sell their house to pay off some creditors, creating even more disruption in the kids' lives. Though they were too young to understand everything that was going on, they knew it all related to money. After all, it was all that their parents seemed to talk about—and argue about—over the course of a year.

Sharon and Dan were happily married parents of two children. On the surface, their extreme money behaviors were less visible than those of the two couples we just profiled. They owned a small graphic design studio that was moderately successful, and their talent combined with their excellent relationship-building skills helped them compete in a tough market. In both their professional and personal lives, Sharon and Dan were good savers and moderate spenders. Their extreme behavior? They weren't interested in the details of money management. They were highly disorganized with their finances both at work and at home, and bills often didn't get paid on time or until they received a few notices and phone calls. Ironically, they got into financial trouble during a time when business was great. They were working such long hours and dealing with so many deadlines that they let things slip. One supplier for their graphic design studio was so frustrated with their inability to pay his bills on a timely basis that he refused to do business with them again. Losing a supplier was bad, but it was even worse when they lost a major customer who was perturbed by their disorganization—they had misplaced at least two checks the customer had sent them and had recently billed him for a service that had not been provided. Even more disturbing, Sharon and Dan were in trouble with the Internal Revenue Service for not only filing a return late but providing inaccurate information. Both of them felt that the world was suddenly coming down on their heads, and they were furious at both themselves for creating the problems and at their customers and the IRS for not understanding that "this is just the way we are." To their credit, Dan and Sharon didn't take out their anger on their kids. They did, however, find themselves spending much less time with their children than they had in the past. To untangle their financial web, they had to spend time and money meeting with lawyers and accountants; they also devoted considerable effort to installing and learning how to use a financial software package. It took more than a year for them to get everything straight, and even when they weren't busy fixing the mess they had made, they were distracted by all their financial woes—they spent a lot of time on the phone both at work and at home talking with friends and family members about all the issues involved. To Dan and Sharon's children, it seemed as if their parents were both obsessed by money. Despite their previously disorganized and disinterested approach, it was now all they seemed to care about.

These three stories are just the tip of the iceberg. You'd be surprised at how many parents are susceptible to extreme money behaviors. It may simply take a specific event or circumstance to push them into an extreme mode. Financially intelligent parents are aware of their vulnerability to these extremes, and this awareness helps them moderate their behaviors. Part of this awareness involves understanding why extreme money behaviors are so enticing to so many people.

WHY WE GO TO EXTREMES

What causes these truly unhealthy behaviors with money? There are a number of reasons, and what's so important for the financially intelligent parent to understand is that many of them are directly linked to the messages we receive about money as we are growing up.

Consider why people compulsively shop. The American Psychological Association estimates that as many as fifteen million Americans are compulsive shoppers who have little control over how much they spend or what they buy. Compulsive shopping is often linked to such factors as emotional deprivation in childhood, a need to fill an internal void and approval seeking. According to therapist April Lane Benson, editor of *I Shop, Therefore I Am,* compulsive shoppers are driven by feelings of low self-esteem, dependency and anxiety. "Said simply," writes Benson, "compulsive buying seems to represent a desperate search for self in people whose identity is neither firmly felt nor dependable." Possessions give these people the sense of identity they didn't get as children. Remember, though, that shopping isn't bad; only compulsive shopping that you can't control is a problem. There is a big difference between buying for self-worth and buying for self-fulfillment—between buying a new computer you don't need simply because it's faster than your neighbor's, and buying a computer to write a novel.

Another likely cause of extreme behaviors is the addictive quality of money. We can become addicted to anything that gives us pleasure. Neurologically speaking, if an activity is pleasurable, doing that activity produces chemicals in our brain known as beta-endorphins, which make us feel good, a feeling similar to the high that runners get. You can become physically addicted to your own brain chemicals and continue engaging in an activity in order to keep getting the high. Overspenders become addicted to the high their behavior with money produces, even though it may have extremely negative consequences, such as going into debt or destroying their marriage.

Misers are the opposite of overspenders, and their extreme actions are motivated by a pathological fear of not having enough. They resist spending money on anything, even though they can afford it. They won't seek medical care for themselves when they are ill. Howard Hughes was a famous miser who wouldn't spend money on proper medical care. While this fear of not having enough may be rooted in childhood experiences, it may also emanate from an adult experience, such as having been through bankruptcy or having barely averted some other financial disaster.

Hoarders are related to misers, in the sense that they hold tightly to things rather than money, and they do so in extreme ways. They harbor an irrational fear that they might need that old fountain pen some day or that their old running shoes might come in handy and that they would forever regret it if they threw them away. One hoarder, a mother of three, bought a store's entire inventory of any items she purchased, whether it was shoes, an outfit or a set of dishes. She owned a home and two rental units. Her home was filled with these purchases. She could no longer rent one of the rental units because it was overflowing with hoarded purchases, and she was getting ready to evict the tenant in the second unit because she needed the additional storage space.

Sometimes the cause of extreme money behaviors is situational. For instance, the stress involved in separation and divorce can push a parent to the far left or right of the money continuum. A parent with a tendency to spend or hoard can go overboard in either direction because he's seeking comfort. Extreme money behavior during separation and divorce can also stem from the desire to punish the spouse who wanted out of the marriage. It is not uncommon for one or both spouses to empty bank accounts, refuse to pay the bill for a child's orthodontia or do any number of things as punishment. In addition, some parents fall into extreme money behaviors after a loved one dies; their grief or inability to grieve properly may cause them to go on spending binges, stop working and take other actions that they normally wouldn't take.

Again, awareness is a good first step to moderate these extreme behaviors. When you recognize what's causing you to hoard, spend compulsively or work obsessively, you are in a much better position to address a specific behavior. When you realize you're using work to comfort yourself or you're hoarding because of irrational fears, you are no longer stuck in an unthinking pattern of behavior. You possess the insight necessary to try to break out of the pattern.

There are many other ways to moderate extreme behaviors. Let's look at some common tools and techniques financially intelligent parents employ.

HOW TO BACK AWAY FROM THE FAR END OF THE CONTINUUM

Financially intelligent parents are proactive about their money behaviors. Not only are they on the lookout for problems that might be negatively impacting their children, but they're willing to do something about them sooner rather than later. All of us are susceptible to some type of extreme behavior, but the financially intelligent among us know enough to back off from these extremes. To help yourself back off, use the following three-step process:

Subject Your Behaviors to the Extreme Litmus Test

Don't jump to conclusions that your money actions and attitudes are at the far side of the continuum, and by the same token, don't assume that just because your behaviors seem normal to you that they're normal to everyone else. A good litmus test to determine whether they fall in the extreme range involves the following:

- ***Have you received feedback from family and friends about a money behavior they find irksome or odd?*** *Has more than one person told you that you are a cheapskate? Have they said they're sick of you complaining that you're one paycheck away from the poorhouse? See if a common theme emerges; if it does, it could indicate an extreme behavior.*
- ***Assess the frequency with which you repeat this behavior.*** *A few times a year is very different from a few times a week. The more often you repeat the behavior, the more likely it is that it falls into the extreme group.*
- ***Watch for a pattern.*** *Extreme money behaviors usually follow a pattern. Typically, a triggering event sets off a familiar money behavior—for instance, something negative happens at work and you immediately go on a shopping spree. Our earlier list of common extreme behaviors can help you identify a pattern.*
- ***Determine whether there is logic to the behavior.*** *By this we mean, is what you're doing reasonable and rational, given the events that preceded it? If you've just lost your job or suffered a serious financial setback, you naturally are going to be very cautious about spending money. If, on the other hand, you experience a financial setback and start spending money, there is no logic to your response. By the same token, think about whether what you're buying is unnecessary or frivolous. All of us make silly purchases on occasion, but when the vast*

majority of your purchases are unnecessary, it may be a sign of problems.

Reflect on Why You Have Fallen into an Extreme Money Pattern

Taking some time to figure out why you use money to buy love or why you find yourself constantly shopping will help you reduce the addictive quality of the behavior. Think about your childhood and your parents' money relationships. Is there a recent stressful event such as divorce or death of a loved one that might be causing you to resort to an extreme way of acting? You might also want to talk about the underlying cause of your behavior with your spouse, close friend or therapist. Unexamined extreme behaviors have the strongest hold on people, and you can loosen their grip a bit when you think and talk about why you fall into them.

Make a Commitment to Moderate These Behaviors Slightly

The good news is that if parents make small changes in their money behaviors, they often can back away from extremes and limit the harm done to their children. Focus on making small, incremental changes rather than large ones.

Beyond these three steps, a variety of other tactics are available to help deal with extreme money behaviors. One technique that some compulsive shoppers find useful in moderating their behavior is *reverse shopping*, a concept we first ran across in a December 2001 article by Patricia Volk in *O, the Oprah Magazine* entitled "Cheap Thrills." Sometimes she goes to a store and says, "What *won't* I buy today?" She finds something she can't live without and then imagines seeing it at her home stuffed in with a lot of other products she doesn't use. Other times she goes through her favorite catalog, folds down the pages for the things she adores, and puts it away for a week. When she looks at it again, she can't figure out what looked so good, tosses the catalog away and thinks of all the time and money she's saved.

Other parents find therapy and support groups helpful to deal with extreme money behaviors. Psychotherapy is available for money disorders on an individual, couples or group basis. Among support groups, Debtors Anonymous (www.debtorsanonymous.org) is a twelve-step program based on the Alcoholics Anonymous model. Its core concept is that debt is an addictive disease and solvency is the solution. Solvency means not incurring any new unsecured debt and is the Debtors Anonymous equivalent of AA's sobriety. The local Debtors Anonymous chapter is often a good source of referrals for qualified psychotherapists in your community. Financial recovery counseling is also available on an individual or couples basis through individual financial counselors. A useful resource in this area is *It's Your Money: Achieving Financial Well-Being* by Karen McCall, available through her Web site, www.financialrecovery.com.

Answer to Financially Intelligent Brainteaser

Answer A may tempt you, especially if you're a reader of this book; we've stressed the importance of using trips to the store to help educate children about marketplace realities. If, however, you're shopping till you drop, you're only making your extreme behavior marginally more acceptable. Answer B is clearly the wrong thing to do, since you're essentially bribing your children to allow you your vice. Answer D is unrealistic; most addicts who try to stop their addiction cold turkey end up falling back into old habits after a period of deprivation. C is the best choice, since moderating the behavior will greatly diminish the negative impact on kids and also provides you with a realistic goal. ◆

11

ENGAGE IN DIFFICULT FINANCIAL DISCUSSIONS

Financially Intelligent Brainteaser

One night at dinner, your ten-year-old son asks you, "Are we rich?" Before you can even think of an answer, he peppers you with a series of related questions, wanting to know how much you make and whether you have more money than his friend's parents—apparently he and his friend engaged in a discussion earlier in the day about whose parents have more money. You decide to answer his queries about your income versus that of his buddy's parents in the following way:

A. We are comfortable, not rich, and we are in a similar financial situation to your friend's parents.

B. It sounds like you're trying to turn this into a contest, and we don't approve of that sort of thing.

C. Why do you want to know? Why is this important to you now?

D. Your friend's parents make more money, but I think we're a much happier family.

(Answer at end of chapter)

To a certain extent, we've examined how to talk to your kids about money via the seven money behaviors discussed in chapters 4–10. Many of you, however, may find certain money-related subjects extremely difficult to discuss with your children. You may discover that you can't talk to them about your salary or what they might inherit or how your investments are doing. Consciously or not, you avoid talking about certain financial topics that make you uncomfortable or that seem too complicated to explain. You may model good money behaviors in certain ways, but unless you complement these behaviors with good money conversations, you're not being as effective a financially intelligent parent as you could be.

Every day brings teachable times that give you the opportunity to talk to your children about a range of financial issues. Putting money in the parking meter, standing in the checkout line and figuring out the tip when you have dinner at a restaurant are all teachable times. Writing out a check to charity, hearing your child request an increase in his allowance and starting a savings account to help pay for college can all set the stage for productive talks about money.

Some people avoid the areas where they have money relationship problems—a chronic overspender may well avoid discussing spending issues with his kids. But you may not be sure precisely why you shy away from these conversations. Be aware, though, that you're not unique in this regard. Most of us find certain money discussions awkward at the very least—we've already drawn the parallel between these discussions and those concerning the birds and the bees—and even if we try to talk with our kids about money, we often don't do a very good job of it.

Financially intelligent parents know why they become tongue-tied around money issues, and we'd like to help you explore what specifically is causing you problems in this area.

THE FOUR VERBAL ROADBLOCKS

Why is it so difficult for you to talk with your child about everything from how much money you have to why she can't have every toy or article of clothing she desires? We've found that most parents are stymied by one or more of the following:

- ***You didn't learn about money when you were growing up.*** *It doesn't matter whether you grew up in a blue-collar neighborhood or in Beverly Hills, California. Chances are your parents never* *talked to you about allowances, materialism or any money-related topic. As a result, you are following in their footsteps.* Born Rich *is a documentary about the lives of several young heirs and heiresses to some of America's greatest fortunes. In one scene, Jamie Johnson, the twenty-three-year-old heir to the Johnson & Johnson pharmaceutical fortune, asks his father why he never talked to him about money or prepared him to manage it responsibly. His father replies, "Money isn't something you talk about in polite society." Our culture, too, has reinforced negative money attitudes; you can see these attitudes in common expressions such as "filthy rich" and "money hungry." In families of all economic levels, money can be a taboo conversational subject. This taboo has a profound effect on people's money attitudes when they grow up, and it may be why you find it difficult to initiate or carry on money talks with your kids.*

- ***You perceived money as something to be feared when you were a child.*** *Emma, for instance, recalled how her father lost his job when she was eleven, her mother had to go back to work to help support the family and they had to move to a smaller house in a neighborhood that wasn't as nice as the one they lived in when she was younger. Today, the subject of money is a major source of anxiety for Emma, and she avoids talking about it with her kids, not wanting to bring back unpleasant memories. Witnessing parents fight over money or experiencing major upheavals as a child because of financial setbacks often contributes to adult financial fears.*

- ***You are currently experiencing money difficulties.*** *Even if your parents exhibited good money behaviors, you may be unable to have money conversations with your kids because of a money problem you've recently experienced. It can be anything from bad investments to a money-management mess, but whatever it is, it makes you want to shun the topic, especially with your kids. You could be worried that they'll view you as a hypocrite if you tell* *them to stick to a budget when you're not very good at this task. Maybe you're sick to death of thinking and talking about money, since it's all you've been thinking and talking about since a given financial crisis occurred.*

- ***You think that there is plenty of time to talk to them about money "later."*** David's only eight; Susie is only six; I've got lots of time to talk to them about money when they get older. *As we like to tell people at our workshops,* later is now. *Don't labor under the mistaken notion that kids can't talk intelligently about money until adolescence. The longer you wait, the more you have to teach them. The longer you wait, the more teachable times you miss when you could have helped them develop a work ethic or learn how to think in terms of choices and alternatives. The longer you wait, the more developmental stages you miss where kids are primed to absorb specific money lessons.*

At certain times, everyone is a bit reluctant to talk about money matters with their kids, and it may have nothing to do with the previous reasons. Sometimes you're tired from work or for other reasons and just can't summon the energy a money discussion requires. Sometimes you may have a legitimate reason not to talk to them—you don't want to alarm them unnecessarily after you just lost your job or you're in the middle of a complex financial mess that would be too difficult for them to understand.

Most of the time, though, people refrain from talking about money with their kids for the wrong reasons. The odds are that at least one of the reasons presented here resonated with you. As we've emphasized throughout this book, when you are aware of the reason behind your behavior, you're that much closer to being able to change it.

THE TOUGHEST QUESTIONS: HOW TO RESPOND TO MONEY QUERIES THAT MAKE YOU UNCOMFORTABLE OR LEAVE YOU TONGUE-TIED

Of course, just knowing why you have difficulty engaging in these conversations isn't the only thing you need. Invariably, kids ask certain types of questions that irritate and discombobulate most parents. If you're like most moms and dads, you'll ignore the questions or respond negatively or angrily. Here are some of the tough questions you've probably already encountered:

"How much money do you make?"

"How much money do we have in the bank?"

"How much is our house worth?"

"Why won't you buy a ___________ for me?"

"Why can't I buy a toy gun? I have the money."

"Why are you so cheap? You never get me anything! I hate you!"

"Mom and Dad, I've maxed out my credit card. Can I have some money to pay for what I want to buy?"

These questions are on-ramps toward productive—albeit sometimes difficult—discussions. Let's look at these questions and the best ways to respond to them.

"Are We Rich?" "How Much Money Do You Make?" and Other Dollar-Specific Questions

Parents are often taken aback by dollar-specific questions. They are afraid that their child will share this private information with others or will feel superior or inferior to other kids. While it's possible that this might happen, it's not a reason to ignore or dismiss the questions; behind them are often legitimate fears and concerns.

For example, Christina, age seven, asked her parents whether they were rich, and when they asked her why she wanted to know, she explained that one of her classmates had said that her father had lost his job and they were going to have to move. "If we're rich," Christina told her parents, "we won't have to move if Daddy loses his job."

Bruce and Diane recently bought a new home. One Sunday morning they were reading the newspaper and their fourteen-year-old son, Ethan, asked, "How much did this house cost?" They looked up and saw that Ethan was holding the real estate section of the local newspaper. Bruce asked Ethan why he was interested and received the typical adolescent response: "Because I want to know." Instead of getting irked, Bruce and Diane treated the question as a teachable time. They told him the purchase price, adding that there were other houses in the neighborhood that cost more and others that cost less, and then engaged him in a discussion of what makes a house a home—how a house is a reflection of the attitudes and actions of the people who live in it, and that the biggest house in the world is worthless if people are rude to each other or don't respect each other. They ended the conversation by reminding him that certain subjects, such as family finances, should stay within the family and not be discussed with others.

Bruce and Diane are financially intelligent parents, and they handled this situation skillfully for two reasons. First, they used a question to engage Ethan in conversation. Responding to a difficult question with a question of your own—rather than a pronouncement—often increases your child's willingness to both talk and listen. Second, they expanded the discussion from money to values. Bruce and Diane used Ethan's curiosity about the value of their house to create a teachable moment where they were able to talk about the intangibles that make up a home: love, caring for one another, sharing responsibilities and so on. By pointing out that there were other houses in the neighborhood that cost less and others that cost more, they were able to talk about the need to keep money in perspective and not to use it as a measure of self-worth. If you learn to treat money only as a scorecard, they told him, you will always be disappointed. Unless you are Bill Gates, there will always be someone with more money than you.

Some of you may be horrified that Bruce and Diane told Ethan how much their home cost. Consider, though, the alternative of not saying anything: instilling anxiety through excessive money secrecy. Think about how this anxiety can affect your child's development. We have worked with financial advisers who tell us that they have clients who are so secretive about their money that they won't reveal their net worth to them; it's like refusing to tell a doctor about your overall physical condition. If your words and your behavior teach that money is a subject to be kept secret, your child may grow into an adult whose money anxiety may cause him to distrust his spouse, much less his financial adviser.

Finally, overcome your reluctance to discuss dollar-specific questions by reminding yourself that your kids probably know more about your finances than you think they do. We live in the information age. You would be amazed, or perhaps aghast, to discover that your kids can find general answers to many dollar-specific questions on the Internet. For example, a few minutes on www.hotjobs.com discloses that the average income of an experienced advertising agency account executive in Fort Wayne, Indiana, ranges from seventy-three thousand to eighty-nine thousand dollars a year, while an experienced tool and die maker in Detroit makes an average of fifty-five thousand to sixty-one thousand dollars per year. In Ethan's case, the real estate section of the local newspaper gave him the asking price for houses in the neighborhood. Refusing to answer Ethan's question when he already had an idea of the range of values would simply tell him that Bruce and Diane were either excessively secretive about money or that they didn't trust him.

"Why Won't You . . . ?" Questions

There is probably no parent on earth who hasn't been asked, "Why won't you buy me a __________?" Typically, these questions are accompanied by such announcements as, "I'm the only kid in my class who doesn't have a __________," and "No other parents have rules like yours!" Depending on your child's age, you can fill in the blank with everything from a candy bar to a new car.

These are difficult conversations to have because you may be reluctant to delve into the sometimes complicated reasons why they can't have a candy bar or a car. Many times, the complexity is due to your values; it requires time and effort to explain why your child can't have a five-hundred dollar bike just like two of his friends; how you believe giving him such a bike fosters a sense of entitlement; how it's not the same thing as giving him a thousand-dollar computer, which he can use as a learning tool, and that you value education while you don't value buying trendy things to be "in." In many cases, the explanation is even more complex and ambiguous than the one just suggested. You may believe that your child isn't able to understand all the issues you might raise or you don't want to get into a long, drawn-out argument.

As a result, many financially *un*intelligent parents rely on the knee-jerk answer, "We can't afford it." Of course, if you really can't afford it, this response is appropriate. Most of the time, though, kids ask for things parents can afford, and to pretend that you can't involves lying to your children as well as taking the easy way out. In addition, repeated reliance on the we-can't-afford-it excuse fosters needless anxiety in children.

Tony and Julie told us that they were dumbfounded a few years ago to receive a phone call from the vice principal of their local school offering to help them apply for the community's financial assistance program. Julie's favorite way of saying no to her eight-year-old son, Max, was telling him that they couldn't afford it. Max became so anxious that he told his teacher that the family was on the verge of bankruptcy!

Maybe your kids are not afraid that the family is about to go bankrupt, but if they see you coming home with a new camera or a new dress after telling them that you can't afford to buy them a computer game, they'll view you as a hypocrite.

The best way to say no, therefore, is to couch your response in a values statement. State your values simply and in a manner that shows how those values relate to the topic at hand. For example:

> *"I don't want to buy that cereal. It isn't healthy because it has too much sugar."*
>
> *"I've already bought you two things you wanted today and that's enough."*
>
> *"I don't want to buy that brand. They have a poor record of child labor. Let's get this brand instead."*
>
> *"I don't want to spend my money on violent computer games."*

Many times, these values statements help start productive conversations about what is important to you and what is important to your child. Your child may not agree with your values—he may not embrace nonviolent principles in the way that you do—but you'll at least help him be aware that you're saying no for a reason and get him to think about this reason. It also will make engaging in the conversation easier for you. Most people are more motivated to talk about tough subjects when they're communicating deeply held beliefs, and attaching your values to the discussion provides this motivation.

"Why Can't I . . . ?" Questions

These questions generally arise when you forbid your child from using her own money to buy something she wants. "Why can't I use my money to get my [choose most any portion of your child's anatomy] pierced?" and "Why can't I get the Slash and Burn video game?" are two examples. Don't make the mistake of responding "Because I say so!" and leaving it at that. Such unilateral, angry answers to your children's questions turn ordinary objects and services into forbidden fruit. Your refusal to discuss the question gives the desired item an allure that it ordinarily wouldn't have and creates the possibility of a power struggle—you defend your decision with a blunt "I'm the parent" and your child complains, "But it's my money!"

Again, respond to these types of questions by explaining how your values prompted your decision. Discuss why you feel the chocolate-covered, marshmallow-embedded, preservative-laced cereal she saw advertised on television flies in the face of a healthy lifestyle. Talk about why a particular song or singer condones violence toward women, and how that goes against your values. Be as specific as possible in your response to your child's question: "I know the squirt gun can't hurt anyone, but it looks like a real automatic weapon, and it's the type of weapon that kills kids your age not more than fifteen miles from where we live."

These discussions are difficult because you feel guilty denying your child's right to use her money as she pleases. It's much easier to just say no (or, for that matter, yes) and avoid dealing with your own mixed feelings about a given issue. If you encourage your child to articulate why she wants a given product and then explain why you're forced to say no based on your values, though, you capitalize on an opportunity to have a productive money discussion.

"Why Are You So Cheap?" Questions

They may not call you cheap, but they clearly imply that the reason you're not getting them what they want is that you don't care enough about them to spend the money. They might add, "You never get me anything! I hate you!" Naturally, your temptation is to shut down the conversation immediately.

Resist the temptation. Recognize that your child has become so emotionally invested in a purchase or an activity that his sense of self is dependent on it. What he's really saying is, "I need [brand name] sneakers to fit in with everybody else," or "If I don't go to Daytona Beach at spring break, I won't be popular." His value systems are linked to advertisements or peers at school rather than to the values you've been teaching at home.

Try to bring the conversation back to the values he learned at home where his sense of self is not a function of what he has but who he is. Let him know that you understand that his sense of self is involved in the request and try to recall concrete examples of times when he held on to family values or came back to them when faced with peer pressure or advertising. Acknowledge his feelings—let him know you realize that he's unhappy that you said no—but allow him to express them, even if they are hurtful toward you. You might also want to remind him of instances when you weren't cheap—when you bought him things he wanted that were aligned with your values.

Perhaps most important, don't respond to his remarks with sarcasm, such as, "Oh, you poor child. You never get anything. You must have been born into the wrong family." Sarcasm repudiates your child's needs. However you may view those needs, they are legitimate to him. Sarcasm is a slap in the face. Resist the impulse to make fun of how he feels.

"I'm Short of Cash; Can I Have Some More Money?" Questions

Parents don't like the conversations resulting from these questions for many reasons, not the least of which is that they are forced to acknowledge that their children are behaving irresponsibly with money—especially when they are older and max out their credit cards. Sometimes it's easier to give in and give them the money they need without discussion. As you can probably guess, this is a big mistake.

Many psychologists and sociologists have observed that children today often take longer than any prior generation to assume adult responsibility. Not only are they marrying and having kids later, but they often take longer to find careers. Perhaps most significantly, they often live at home with their parents (sometimes moving out and then moving back in when cash runs low) into their mid-twenties. In 1960, 43 percent of young adults between the ages of eighteen and twenty-four were living at home. By 1990 the percentage rose to 52.8 percent.

As a result, when your children start approaching adulthood, money conversations tend to become more complicated. Your almost-adult is caught between the advantages and disadvantages of becoming financially independent, and while she may want the social freedom that comes with being on her own, she may also enjoy living rent-free in a nice home with good food and cable television. Caroline, for instance, moved back to her parents' home when she was laid off by an ad agency. At age twenty-four and after two years of working, she had saved nothing and maxed out two credit cards. Over the course of the next year, she frequently asked her parents for money, which they gave to her; they were overjoyed to have their only daughter back home and figured she'd be back on her feet soon. In reality, being at home was safe and comfortable, and she had little incentive to get back on her feet. She made only a few feeble attempts to find work and kept telling her parents that she wanted to keep her options open in case the ad agency called her back. After a year, Caroline's parents wanted to confront her about how she was sleeping until noon, partying frequently and making little effort to find work. When Caroline next asked them for money, they tried to talk to her about it, but she immediately burst into tears and went off on a rant about how she was going through a difficult time—she had boyfriend problems on top of her financial woes—and that if they just gave her a little time and money, she'd work things out on her own. They were reluctant to bring up the topic again, and the last we heard, Caroline was still living at home.

Admittedly, these can be incredibly difficult conversations both to initiate and to sustain. Here are a few things you can do that will help when your almost-adult child hits you up for more money:

Reorganize the Way You View Your Adult Child. Social psychologist Terri Apter, author of *The Myth of Maturity*, points out that this lengthening transition between adolescence and adulthood creates a seeming paradox that parents must understand. To become adults, our children must pull away from us and learn to make their own decisions. The increased time it takes to become a truly independent adult means that our adult children need our emotional and psychological support more than ever. Too often we find it difficult to distinguish between curtailing financial support for our adult children and curtailing emotional support for them. While reducing or even eliminating financial support may be appropriate, it is vital that you continue to provide your young adult with emotional support. Your conversations, therefore, should be filled with emotional support, a much more valuable gift to your child than financial assistance.

Listen More Than You Talk. When your near-adult tells you about running short of money and wanting to borrow some, don't automatically tell him what to do. Listening is more important than talking. Offer advice rather than directions; help him build self-confidence by letting him make decisions and take charge of his life. Ask him what his options are for making money and listen as he tells you about his hopes and dreams.

Share Your Own Struggles. Our kids often enter adulthood with unrealistic optimism and return home when they discover they don't like scrimping and saving and living in a style to which they're not accustomed. Help them understand that they're not the only ones who have had to deal with this situation. Perhaps you lived at home at some point when you were a young adult. Perhaps you got yourself in financial trouble as a near-adult. When your child tells you her tale of woe and asks for money, share your own story of how you struggled. It demonstrates that if you can make it, she can, too.

Finally, some people find it easier to "discuss" this difficult financial issue in writing. Therefore, take a cue from one of our workshop attendees. Al Wroblewski, an independent financial planner in Cambridge, Massachusetts, who tries to "practice what he preaches," shared a copy of a letter he had written to his adult children about providing them with financial assistance. We like to call it the "Endeavors" letter. Al said that he was willing to help them financially by "supporting worthwhile endeavors." He said that in evaluating requests for money, he was looking at several things:

- *Is whatever you're going to do important to you? Are you really committed?*
- *Does it represent something meaningful both to yourself and to others?*
- *Does it move you toward financial self-sufficiency?*
- *Will money make a difference?*
- *Is giving you money healthy for our relationship?*

The letter ended with this observation, which perhaps really says it all: "The distinction I guess I would like to draw between giving you money for worthwhile endeavors versus just for the hell of it is the difference between using money I give you to fuel your independence versus using it to prolong your dependency or to take the easy way out."

Answer to Financially Intelligent Brainteaser

At first, answer A may seem correct since it's a civilized response. At the same time, though, it is really a nonresponse and doesn't capitalize on your child's curiosity or invite him to explore his feelings about wealth. Answer B makes him feel bad for asking the question and stifles discussion; it's a common response for parents who have grown up with taboos around money issues. Answer D is probably the worst choice, since it suggests a parent who feels inferior because he doesn't make as much money as the other parent; he is communicating that happiness is more important than money, but he's doing so in a way that suggests that wealthy people are unhappy. The correct answer, therefore, is C. As we've emphasized, asking a question in response to this type of money question can help your child explore his beliefs and values about money. ◆

12

FLEXIBILITY: HOW TO INTEGRATE THE BEHAVIORS INTO YOUR PARENTING STYLE

All of us want what's best for our kids, but when faced with money issues, we often don't know how to get there or even where *there* is. If you're like most parents we work with, you want to do the right thing, but no one has ever taught you what the right thing is. There is plenty of information out there about how to be a good parent but, until now, precious little material about how to be a financially intelligent parent.

As a result, many of you rely on your instincts to guide your behaviors. Unfortunately, your instincts may be rooted in your childhood relationship with money, which causes you to make money decisions that feel right for you but are wrong for your kids.

The eight money behaviors suggested in this book, therefore, are good reality checks for your instincts. It may be that the behaviors and your instincts are in harmony. If they're not, though, the behaviors provide you with some alternatives. Ideally, you will be able to integrate these eight behaviors into your parenting style. Practically speaking, this integration takes time and effort. Most important, it takes flexibility.

RECOGNIZE YOUR RIGIDITY

If you start employing some of the ideas and techniques we've suggested in these pages, you're likely to encounter some resistance—from yourself! As you attempt to talk with your children about taboo money subjects, give them an allowance for the first time or involve the family in charitable projects, you may feel anxious, insecure, angry or fearful. As a result, you may return to traditional money-behavior patterns that make you feel much more comfortable. If this happens, understand that any change—even a small amount—creates some discomfort. Go slowly, grit your teeth and remind yourself that you need to break the pattern. When you see your child responding positively—becoming less materialistic or more willing to think about his own money behaviors before acting—the discomfort will ease.

Recognize your rigidity. Be alert for reactions suggesting you are digging in rather than considering alternatives. To recognize rigid behavior, ask yourself:

- *Am I being extremely stubborn on this issue for a reason I can articulate? Is the reason in accordance with my values?*
- *If I can't articulate the reason, have I acted like this in the past in similar situations?*
- *Does even the thought of changing this particular behavior make me anxious or angry?*
- *Do I find that even trying to make a slight change in my traditional response causes me to feel uncomfortable and makes me want to return to my former rigid response?*

Sometimes, parents are inflexible about money for good reason. They absolutely forbid their children to buy violent video games or take a summer job with a company that exploits its employees. Many times, though, the reasons for being financially rigid have nothing to do with values and everything to do with a parent's own relationship with money. Here are some common examples of money-related rigidity:

- *refusing every request your child makes for an increase in allowance, automatically assuming the reason is invalid*

- *using every excuse you can think of to avoid participating with your child in a charitable event or activity*
- *insisting on monitoring every penny spent by your child, even if he demonstrates responsibility and trustworthiness*
- *refusing to discuss certain money topics, either by decreeing them off-limits or by steering the conversation in other directions*
- *punishing your child excessively for relatively minor money infractions (e.g., grounding your child for a week because he spent five dollars more on clothes than you had agreed upon)*
- *expecting your kids to contribute most of the money they make from a job to the family because that's exactly what was expected of you as a child*
- *responding to a child's financial mistake with a lecture you've delivered a hundred times before*
- *expecting your child to spend, acquire and manage money exactly as you do*

All parents exhibit some of these rigid behaviors at times. Financially intelligent parents, though, learn to resist their rigid impulses. In this way, they are better able to integrate the eight money behaviors into their parenting style.

WHAT YOUR CHILD GAINS FROM YOUR FLEXIBILITY

Ultimately, you want to raise a child who is financially and emotionally responsible, who is willing and able to give to others (and not just take) and who has a strong work ethic. Flexibility isn't a magic wand and won't grant all these wishes, but it will help you adjust your money behaviors when they're pushing your child away from attaining these admirable qualities.

The good news is that you can adjust no matter what age your child is or how long you've been persisting in financially *un*intelligent behaviors. We'd like to share two stories of parents who used flexibility in positive ways.

Mia and Jordan, a couple who attended one of our workshops, had been married for twelve years and had two daughters, ages seven and nine. Neither of them believed in giving their daughters an allowance; they simply bought them what they wanted. Both Mia and Jordan had grown up in families that didn't have much money. When they became parents, they vowed to give their kids whatever they needed, and they didn't believe an allowance was necessary to achieve this goal. Over time, though, they became concerned because their kids sometimes acted entitled. On one occasion, Mia heard their older daughter tell a friend that "my mom and dad will get me anything I want." In addition, when they received presents, they seemed to take the gifts for granted, offering insincere thank-yous or not bothering to hide their disappointment if gifts didn't meet their expectations.

After attending our workshop, however, Mia and Jordan made an effort to be more flexible, and that included trying an allowance on an "experimental basis." Though neither was convinced that an allowance was a good idea, they agreed that they needed to do something differently. At first, Mia and Jordan were skeptical when they handed their daughters a weekly sum of money; they felt that they were imposing needless restrictions on their kids, and it brought back uncomfortable memories from their own childhoods. After a month, though, they saw positive results. Their daughters had to learn how to delay gratification and save money for a goal. Perhaps even more important, the allowance provided Mia and Jordan with natural topics for family money discussions. Each week, they talked to their children about how they were spending their allowances, the high cost of certain desirable products and services and the need to think long term if they wanted to buy them for themselves. Gradually, Mia and Jordan became more comfortable with giving their daughters an allowance, especially as their children's sense of entitlement diminished. The children became gracious takers and generous givers. As Mia and Jordan practiced more of the money behaviors discussed in these pages—an effort that was only possible because of their conscious flexibility—their daughters began to give and receive gifts in a more emotionally mature manner. They didn't have to be reminded that it was someone's birthday and that they should make a gift or card for that individual, and when they received presents, they made the giver feel appreciated.

Flexibility is important for parents not only when kids are young, but even when they're teenagers and young adults. Sabrina was nineteen when we met her mother, Jennifer, a single mother in her forties. Sabrina had dropped out of community college because it was "boring" and was living at home, being supported by Jennifer. For Jennifer, supporting her daughter seemed perfectly appropriate. She told her friends that she, like Sabrina, was a bit lost when she was a young adult and had to struggle to survive financially. Jennifer was very firm in her belief that she would support Sabrina until her daughter "got her act together."

After a few conversations with us, Jennifer realized that her inflexible attitude was doing Sabrina more harm than good. In fact, it was preventing her from facing reality and developing a work ethic. Jennifer decided to tell Sabrina that if she wasn't going to college and wanted to live at home, she needed to get a full-time job within ninety days and she would be expected to contribute to the expenses of running the household. Sabrina responded to her mother's decision with anger and accusations: "This is a tough time in my life; if you really understood me, you'd be there for me with no conditions and no questions asked." Jennifer acknowledged her daughter's anger but said that she had given the matter a lot of thought, and she believed this would be best for Sabrina in the long run. In the short run, of course, there was an escalation of tension between mother and daughter. Sabrina, though, acquiesced to her mom's request, found a full-time job in sales at the local mall and contributed a portion of her salary for household expenses. Sabrina's self-esteem improved once she had a job where she was appreciated and she no longer saw herself as a freeloader at home. After about a year of full-time work, Sabrina mentioned to her mom that she was thinking about going back to school and getting a degree in education. Jennifer and Sabrina had a number of productive discussions about the pros and cons of being a teacher, and Jennifer felt they were some of the best discussions she and her daughter had ever had. Jennifer agreed to pay for Sabrina's college education, and Sabrina is now working part-time and has successfully completed her second year of college. She is convinced that teaching is her true calling.

Flexibility also confers another benefit on kids: It helps them become resilient. When you model flexibility, you teach your kids that it's wise to consider other options, that even if you fail in one approach, another one is available that might be more successful. All of us meet adversity from time to time. Our kids will meet adversity in school, socially, at sports and in many other areas. Later on, they may encounter problems in a job, in a marriage or as the manager of their own finances. If you've been inflexible with your kids, they will be less able to adapt situationally and change their approach when they encounter adversity. People who are flexible and resilient can change directions and get out of financial trouble or adopt a more meaningful lifestyle.

Throughout *The Financially Intelligent Parent*, we've advocated talking with your kids about money issues, but these conversations require flexibility on your part. If you're rigid and unyielding about your money beliefs, you're going to turn conversations into lectures and fail to create dialogues that encourage your children to reflect on the values behind their actions. Keep your money conversations spontaneous and creative. Encourage your kids to think for themselves and develop their own financial judgments. Prompt them to analyze their own behaviors and reflect on decisions they make. Empower them to come to their own conclusions about money and the issues and beliefs related to it.

Developmental psychologist Edith Grotberg, PhD, the author of *A Guide to Promoting Resilience in Children: Strengthening the Human Spirit,* has identified several sources that children use to build resilience. Interestingly, there are clear parallels with the money behaviors of financially intelligent parents:

- *setting limits so that your child knows when to stop before there is danger or trouble (learning to moderate extreme money behaviors)*
- *showing your child how to do things right through your modeling behavior (developing a work ethic)*
- *teaching your child to show concern and be glad to be able to help others (being a charitable family)*
- *teaching your child to be responsible for what she does (learning to think reflectively)*
- *helping your child learn to find ways to solve problems that she faces (reflective thinking plus learning financial responsibility)*
- *teaching your child to control herself when she feels like doing something not right or dangerous (learning to use money in ways consistent with your values)*

PUTTING THE EIGHT BEHAVIORS INTO PRACTICE: BE OPEN TO THE OPPORTUNITIES FOR TEACHING THAT LIFE PRESENTS

You're not going to be able to adopt the eight money behaviors unless you are open-minded, creative and willing to think situationally. There isn't just one way to encourage a work ethic or a single situation conducive to teaching financial reflection. A great deal is going to depend on who you are, who your kids are and the situations that life presents you with.

Years ago we lived near a couple with three kids, two dogs and little insight about their money behaviors. Their dogs were constantly escaping from the backyard by sliding out under the gate. Time after time the family went around the neighborhood looking for the dogs, but they never fixed the gate; they intended to but never got around to it. One day the dogcatcher found the dogs loose and took them to the pound. It cost the couple almost three hundred dollars in fines to get their dogs back, and they complained about the cost for months. It would have cost them less to have fixed the gate. Think of the money message their behavior was sending their kids: *"Don't think ahead about consequences; just complain about them after they occur."*

If the couple had possessed the flexibility we're advocating, they would have spent the money for the gate and demonstrated to their children that the price of prevention was far less than the price of inaction. Or if they didn't fix the gate, they would have explained to their children that they had made a mistake and they were paying the penalty for procrastination. Or they would have turned fixing the gate into an extra chore and paid their kids to do it. In any case, the money message would have been positive.

Think for a moment about how you would react to the following situations:

- *A relative dies and leaves each of your children fifty thousand dollars, and your kids immediately list all the things they want to buy.*
- *Your high school student comes home from school and excitedly tells you about a program that will cost you only twenty-five hundred dollars to send him to a rural location in India for eight weeks where he can help with public health projects.*
- *You are getting a divorce and your children want to know whether you're going to have to sell the house and whether they can continue to take tennis lessons.*

Financially intelligent parents are willing to think creatively about the best ways to handle these situations. When it comes to emotionally charged money issues, parents sometimes act before they think. Consider the different ways you might respond to a given money situation instead of going with your first impulse. For example, if your kids inherit fifty thousand dollars, you can help them consider donating a portion of their inheritance to a charity they resonate with. If they want to go to India to volunteer for eight weeks, suggest that they first participate with a public health organization in your community to see if they enjoy that type of volunteerism. If you are the midst of a divorce, reassure your children that they're loved and be honest if everyone will likely have to make some financial changes. Be flexible and use your imagination and creativity rather than reacting emotionally to issues involving money.

USING MONEY AS A TOOL: A RESOURCE LIMITED ONLY BY YOUR IMAGINATION

Though we've recommended specific behaviors and techniques, you shouldn't feel limited by our recommendations. The eight money behaviors are only a starting point. You may come up with a ninth or tenth behavior that is in keeping with the spirit of the other eight. You may create an approach to foster reflective thinking in your child that works better for you than anything we've suggested. If you do, send us an e-mail so we can share your success with others!

Being a financially intelligent parent isn't about following a formula. Instead, it's about making a commitment to be mindful about money, to be conscious of your financially related words and actions. Once you make this commitment and put forth a consistent effort to model sound money behaviors, you possess great latitude to do it your way. Some of you are going to get your family more involved in charitable work than in practicing the other behaviors. Some of you are going to focus more on stimulating reflective thinking or building a work ethic. Some of you will concentrate on helping your children become financially responsible.

However you choose to implement the ideas in this book, keep in mind that we live in a society where kids can easily lose sight of what really matters. As parents, we must help our kids learn that money is something they have, not something they are. They need to develop the values to deal with money issues constructively and responsibly. These are challenging and difficult goals. *The Financially Intelligent Parent* provides you with a hands-on, positive strategy to accomplish them.

Big goals are achieved by taking small steps, and we'd like to leave you with a story that illustrates this point. We asked our friend Joel to read the various drafts of *The Financially Intelligent Parent*, soliciting his advice about some of the issues we were raising. One evening, Joel sent us the following e-mail, which captures how we hope this book will help parents:

> *Last night, my wife, Lisa, our three-year-old daughter, Sarah, and I were having dinner. Sarah announced that she could identify the letters in her name. She went ahead and spelled out "S a r a h." Lisa and I were delighted and my first reaction was to reach into my pants pocket to give her some coins to put in her piggy bank. All of a sudden I flashed on* The Financially Intelligent Parent *and thought "What am I doing?" I realized that I was teaching Sarah to think of money as a reward! Instead of giving her the money, I hugged her and kissed her and told her how wonderful it was that she knew how to spell her name. She hugged me and kissed me back.*

BIBLIOGRAPHY

Acuff, Dan S., and Robert H. Reiher. *What Kids Buy and Why: The Psychology of Marketing to Kids*. New York: Free Press, 1997.

Apter, Terri. *The Myth of Maturity: What Teenagers Need from Parents to Become Adults*. New York: W.W. Norton, 1999.

Benson, April Lane, ed. *I Shop, Therefore I Am: Compulsive Buying and the Search for Self*. New York: Rowman & Littlefield, 2000.

Brazelton, T. Berry, and Stanley Greenspan. *The Irreducible Needs of Children: What Every Child Must Have to Grow, Learn and Flourish*. Cambridge, MA: Perseus Books, 2000.

Bredehoft, David, et al. "No Rules, Not Enforcing the Rules, No Chores, + Lots of Freedom = Overindulgence Too," Educarer. http://www.educarer.com/oi-structure.htm.

Bredehoft, D.J., et al. "Perceptions Attributed to Parental Overindulgence During Childhood." *Journal of Family and Consumer Sciences Education*, vol. 16, no. 2, Fall/Winter 1998.

Chatzky, Jean. *You Don't Have to Be Rich: Comfort, Happiness, and Financial Security on Your Own Terms*. New York: Penguin Group, 2003.

Coles, Robert. *The Moral Intelligence of Children: How to Raise a Moral Child.* New York: Random House, 1997.

Csikszentmihalyi, Mihaly. *Flow: The Psychology of Optimal Experience*. New York: Harper Collins, 1990.

Dominguez, Joe. *Your Money or Your Life: Transforming Your Relationship with Money and Achieving Financial Independence*. New York: Penguin Books, 1999.

Erikson, E. *Identity and the Life Cycle.* New York: W.W. Norton, 1980.

Gallo, Eileen, and Jon Gallo. *Silver Spoon Kids: How Successful Parents Raise Responsible Children.* Chicago: Contemporary Books, 2002.

Gray, John. *Children Are from Heaven: Positive Parenting Skills for Raising Cooperative, Confident and Compassionate Children.* New York: Harper Collins, 1999.

Greenspan, Stanley I. *The Secure Child: Helping Our Children Feel Safe and Confident in an Insecure World.* Cambridge, MA: Perseus Books, 2002.

Grotberg, Edith. *A Guide to Promoting Resilience in Children: Strengthening the Human Spirit.* Early Childhood Development: Practice and Reflections series. Bernard Van Leer Foundation. http://resilnet.uiuc.edu/library/grotb95b.html#chapter1.

Guthrie, Elisabeth, and Kathy Matthews. *The Trouble with Perfect: How Parents Can Avoid the Overachievement Trap and Still Raise Successful Children.* New York: Broadway Books, 2002.

Hallowell, Edward M. *The Childhood Roots of Adult Happiness: Five Steps to Help Kids Create and Sustain Lifelong Joy.* New York: Ballantine Books, 2002.

Leder, Steven Z. *More Money Than God: Living a Rich Life Without Losing Your Soul.* Chicago: Bonus Books, 2003.

Littwin, Susan. *The Postponed Generation: Why American Youth Are Growing Up Later.* New York: William Morrow, 1986.

Manning, Robert D. *Credit Card Nation: The Consequences of America's Addiction to Credit.* New York: Basic Books, 2000.

McMillon, Bill. *Volunteer Vacations: Short-Term Adventures That Will Benefit You and Others*, 7th ed. Chicago: Chicago Press Review, 1999.

Owen, David. *The First National Bank of Dad: The Best Way to Teach Kids About Money.* New York: Simon & Schuster, 2003.

Pipher, Mary. *The Shelter of Each Other: Rebuilding Our Families.* New York: Ballantine Books, 1996.

Poulter, Stephen B. *Father Your Son: How to Become the Father You've Always Wanted to Be.* New York: McGraw-Hill, 2004.

Siegel, Daniel J., and Mary Hartzell. *Parenting from the Inside Out: How a Deeper Self-Understanding Can Help You Raise Children Who Thrive.* New York: Penguin Putnam, 2003.

Wilmes, David. *Parenting for Prevention: How to Raise a Child to Say No to Alcohol and Other Drugs.* Center City, MN: Johnson Institute/Hazelden, 1995.

Yablonsky, L. *The Emotional Meaning of Money.* New York: Gardner Press, 1991.

Zollo, Peter. *Wise Up to Teens: Insights to Marketing and Advertising to Teens.* New York: New Strategist Publications, 1999.

INDEX

D